THE GREAT RESIGNATION

THE GREAT RESIGNATION

Why Millions Are Leaving Their Jobs and Who Will Win the Battle for Talent

RUSS HILL
JARED JONES

.

THE GREAT RESIGNATION: Why Millions Are Leaving Their Jobs and Who Will Win the Battle for Talent

ISBN:

First Edition

Cover design:
Interior design: Adina Cucicov

TABLE OF CONTENTS

The era of adult daycare is over. The way we work has permanently changed.

INTRODUCTION

It was the strangest feeling. I woke up and stared at the bedroom ceiling. For the first time since becoming an adult, I didn't have a job. My identity had no connection to any company. I had no boss. No employer. No salary. No benefits.

My head rested on a pillow. A thin sheet covered me. My mind raced. "Shouldn't I feel scared? Do I feel scared? Why don't I feel scared? Oh, wow, this is freaking weird," I thought.

I did a quick emotional diagnosis. "What feelings am I experiencing?" I asked myself silently. Joy. Like lots of joy. Relief. And free. Completely and finally free.

Less than twenty-four hours earlier, I left the consulting firm I had worked at for the better part of the last decade. My colleagues were friends. My job involved my passion. COVID-19 had rocked our industry and transformed our company. But 2020 had been my best year ever at the firm—revenue wise. I was one of the top three highest performers with clients including three of the Fortune 10 (the ten biggest companies in the US as measured by revenue). The success I had enjoyed wasn't just measured financially. I had coauthored two books in twelve months. For the first time in my life, books with my name on them were selling on Amazon to people around the world. And week after week, thousands of executives were logging into live virtual sessions I and two of my colleagues were doing.

Life was good. Really good. But I needed a change.

COVID-19 deeply affected me. Not the virus as much as the massive shifts that accompanied it. In the three years before the pandemic, I had boarded 424 flights. March 2020 was scheduled to be my busiest travel month ever. Business trips to Europe, Asia, and across the US were all booked. Then people started getting sick, and the world locked down. My recently graduated son, who had just moved to Australia, was suddenly on a chartered jet bringing Americans back home. My other three kids were spaced out across the house on laptops and iPads, figuring out how to use Zoom. Our gym was closed. Church was cancelled. Streets were empty. Shopping center parking lots were empty of cars by 8 p.m. Restaurants required curbside pickup. And a friend broke down crying during a call from his hospital room. He had been in our home just a few days before, which made us very concerned.

Now, almost a year into the pandemic, I woke up confident that a major lifestyle change was exactly what I needed. Living beneath our means for decades provided space and time to figure out what was next. As I got up out of bed and headed for the shower, my phone rang. The caller was someone I knew well but hadn't talked to in years. "Hey Russ! Do you have a few minutes?" he asked. The CEO of the North American division of a global manufacturing company started detailing problems at a plant. "I need to know what's happening there. Can you get there in the next two weeks?" he asked.

I informed him I was no longer at the consulting firm he knew I worked at. "I don't care. Can you help me?" he asked.

"Absolutely," I responded. We had a signed agreement a few days later. Within days, there would be others. Within weeks, a company was created, and revenue was adding up.

This isn't a book about entrepreneurship. It's not about fleeing the corporate world and starting your own thing. Some of you are considering doing that, and we'll address that trend on some of the pages that follow. This book is about more than that, though. It's about needing a change. You see, I'm not alone. In fact, just wait till we show you the charts of how many people are wondering if it's time to mix things up—professionally. Millions of them are like me and have already acted on that feeling. Tons more will.

This shift that's happening in the workforce didn't begin with the highly contagious virus that temporarily shut down the world. It's a fire that's been burning for a while. The pandemic was just a massive reservoir of gasoline flowing into that fire. Things changed when everyone—or almost everyone—was sent home.

THE GREAT RESIGNATION

We didn't invent the phrase "The Great Resignation." We'll introduce you to the person who did in a few pages. When he uttered those words, he was predicting what might happen. He was making a guess based on data he was seeing in early 2021. We used his phrase as the title of this book because his prediction came true. The numbers are stunning. The movement happening in the workforce is unprecedented. We discovered remarkable data when we went looking for better responses to clients who were asking how to deal with significant shortages of workers and pushback to their back-to-office plans.

Jared: I should probably pipe in here at this point and add a little of my own experience before having Russ set up the rest of the intro to the book. A few months after Russ woke up having become part of The Great Resignation, I joined him. After nearly two decades working at the firm where we were colleagues, I departed as well. I needed a change. Russ and I have since joined forces and cofounded Lone Rock Consulting. Working alongside one of your best friends is pretty cool. Co-owning a company that coaches executives at some of the biggest companies in the world is even cooler. These executives lead retail giants, defense contractors, insurance companies, pharmaceuticals, restaurant chains, hospital systems, energy giants, and car manufacturers.

We're not flexing. We're providing context. On these pages we'll share what we've seen in boardrooms and ballrooms the last two decades that we now realize was the beginning of the shift that's now gaining speed. We'll mix our stories with data from people and institutions who are experts at employment trends and geek out at data that's affecting all of you. We'll mostly use the word "we" in this book. When it's something brilliant, just know chances are I said it. Ok, now back to Russ for the rest of the book's intro...

Russ: I'm rethinking this coauthor thing after that last comment, but I'll pretend I didn't hear it. We'll try to insert a little humor here and there, by the way. The topic of this book is weighty, so hopefully you don't mind a little sarcasm. Okay, back to serious mode:This book is for leaders. Leaders of companies setting strategy designed to gain a competitive advantage during a very different-looking era of work. This book is for leaders of teams. Leaders who are concerned about holding onto their best people and making smart choices for their own career growth. This book is for anyone who can feel the change in the wind, but isn't sure exactly what has shifted or how to adapt to it.

To be honest, this book is designed to be a wakeup call for anyone leading others. What we're about to show you will change the way you view your role.

It will inform and empower you to recruit and retain the brightest and most successful people in your industry.

We know . . . that sounds ambitious. Pretty lofty promises, right? What you're about to see we've presented to executives of some of the world's biggest companies. Their reaction gives us the confidence you're sensing. In other words, we're pretty sure this is a book you need to read.

Before we dig in, we need to do a little pre-framing. What we're going to show you will be useless if you don't receive it in a way that motivates you to act. Even if you only read a couple chapters, we want you better prepared and more empowered to succeed in this new environment. The way we work has changed. The way you lead must as well.

THE CHANGE SEQUENCE®

When my son was sent home from Australia and found his plans dramatically altered, I felt the need, as his dad, to help him process what he was feeling and experiencing. I showed him this model we call *The Change Sequence*. We feel the need to show it to you before we walk you through the magnitude and scope of The Great Resignation and how it will affect you.

When change happens—any kind of change—our natural response is to **mourn**. This happens after anything from the death of a loved one to an unexpected setback at work. Anytime unexpected change happens, we mourn the way it used to be or what we had hoped would happen. How long does mourning typically last? How long should it last? There's no right answer to those questions, right? It depends on the magnitude of the change and the nature of it. Some people are still mourning a divorce or job loss that happened decades ago.

None of us had experienced a change in our lifetime as globally impactful as the COVID-19 pandemic. If we're honest, we've all mourned some aspect of the change we've experienced. Some of you have experienced the death of someone profoundly important to you from this most unpredictable virus. Others have lost your jobs. Some of you have chosen to change careers. And almost all of you have had your personal and professional routines altered permanently.

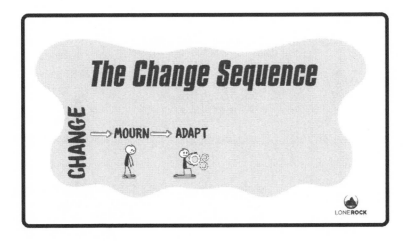

At some point, after we have been mourning whatever change we've experienced, we begin to **adapt.** Adapting is a choice. It is an acknowledgment that the past will never return, and the future requires something different from us. The faster we can begin to transition from the Mourning Stage to the Adapting Stage, the healthier we and the people around us will be. Adapting shifts our focus and energy to gaining strength. You know it's happening when you begin focusing on what you can control and impact. Resentment, frustration, and denial give way to acceptance, ideation, and innovation. Leaders who minimize the amount of time they spend mourning change have tremendous competitive advantage. Their teams and companies thrive in an era dominated by fast-changing customer demands and habits and significant shifts in employee expectations and behavior.

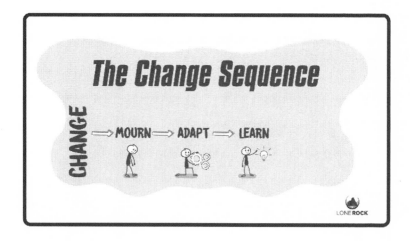

When I introduced this model to my son shortly after he was sent back to the states from Australia, I tried to impress on him that wisdom is optional. The **learning** on the other side of change isn't guaranteed. It has to be captured. Plenty of people experience unexpected change and completely miss the lessons it offers. In the case of my son, I encouraged him to spend some quiet time reflecting on what he had learned from the turmoil he had experienced.

We did the same with a senior executive of a Fortune 100 food services company. His division supplied hotels, universities, and restaurants, selling everything from bacon to party platters. The demand for their products evaporated when all three shut down for months. His team went through the first two phases of The Change Sequence. First, they mourned. How could they not? Everyone's income was affected. They had been beating plan, and then suddenly an unexpected virus wiped out large bonuses and commission checks. We watched as that mourning quickly transitioned into adapting. They established Critical Expectations for their hundreds of sales reps as they searched for customers in new segments.

After most of the initial turmoil of the pandemic had passed and the team was back on solid footing, we were on a call with this executive. He had a virtual meeting coming up soon with his leadership team where they would be reviewing how the year ended up. We asked him to share with us on our call three things he hoped his team had learned from the massive change they had experienced. For the next thirty minutes, he built out that list of three words that captured what he would present the next week to his team. Capturing that learning was their competitive advantage going into the new fiscal year. They didn't stop and celebrate after moving from the Mourn Phase to the Adapt Phase. They made sure they paused and captured their hard-earned wisdom.

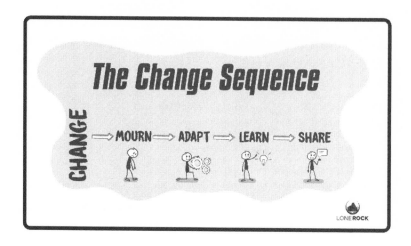

After we learn something new, what is our natural desire? To share it. Effective leaders develop their team by making sure they complete this sequence. They **share** the learning experienced from going through change. The market for wisdom is enormous. Unfortunately, most leaders—most people—only complete one or two steps of this process. The advantages come in making sure we spend time on the last two. It's what the food services executive did in the meeting with his leadership team when he shared their three learnings from 2020.

We wanted to lay this foundation and get you thinking about each of these steps as we walk through the data of the massive shifts happening in the global workforce. The numbers and stories in the next several chapters will reveal the breadth and scope of the change that's happening. It's massive. All of you are experiencing it. Some are stuck mourning the change. You can't wait for things to return to how they used to be. Others are deep in the Adapt Phase. This book is designed to push more of you that direction. Our intent is also to help you learn. To see the macro trends and to help you process specific insights needed for your industry, company, and team. And then we hope you'll share. Share what you find in this book with your team, peers, and friends. We'll share various ways to do that on the pages ahead.

Our purpose in writing this book is to give you a competitive advantage. To help you attract and retain the very best talent. To encourage you to spend a little more energy and mind space on areas we think you might not be focused on. Ultimately, we want to help you lead in a way that accelerates your team's ability to deliver the results that matter most, and, in the process, grows your opportunity to influence others at scale.

PART ONE

WHAT'S CHANGED

CHAPTER ONE

THE SEISMIC SHIFT

Most professors would be jealous of his rating on the Rate My Professor website. When students were asked, "Would you take his course again?" 100 percent said yes. Granted, the sample size wasn't very big. But if his classes were boring or brutal, the dissatisfied students would have been motivated to destroy him online.

Dr. Anthony Klotz teaches at the Mays Business School at Texas A&M University. He landed there after stints at Oregon State and the University of Oklahoma. The guy who used to clock in at the General Mills plant in Albuquerque where they make Trix went on to become an academic who now geeks out on employment data. While you're swiping through Instagram Stories, he's studying data on why people leave their jobs.

It's no surprise Klotz's phone rang when Arianne Cohen needed an expert opinion. She was writing an article for *Bloomberg Businessweek* on how the COVID-19 pandemic was affecting employment trends. Dr. Klotz took the call.

"A great resignation is coming," Klotz told Cohen. He shared some data that had recently come from the US Bureau of Labor Statistics. Cohen listened, but she already had what she needed. She had scored a quote that would be the ultimate clickbait. It wasn't long before the Bloomberg Businessweek website published an article with a big, bold headline predicting a "post-pandemic resignation boom." In that article, the phrase "The Great Resignation" was born.

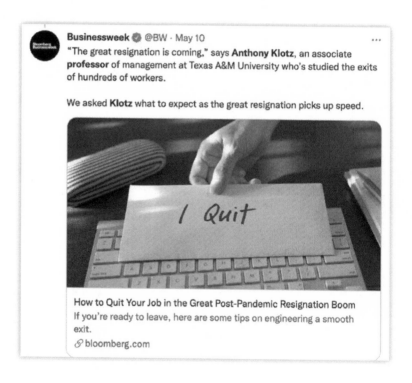

Businessweek ✔ @BW · May 10   •••
"The great resignation is coming," says **Anthony Klotz**, an associate **professor** of management at Texas A&M University who's studied the exits of hundreds of workers.

We asked **Klotz** what to expect as the great resignation picks up speed.

I Quit

How to Quit Your Job in the Great Post-Pandemic Resignation Boom
If you're ready to leave, here are some tips on engineering a smooth exit.
🔗 bloomberg.com

"I was talking to a number of individuals, who, over the last year, had these realizations that they wanted to do something different with their lives," Klotz said. The things he was hearing from friends and colleagues combined with the employment data he was seeing convinced Klotz that something big was on the horizon.

Microsoft saw it too.

The resurging tech company surveyed thirty thousand workers around the globe. They wanted to know how COVID-19 had impacted the world's workforce. One number jumped out at the researchers working on the project. 41 percent!

Forty-one percent of their sample said they were considering leaving their job in the next twelve months. Salespeople in Minneapolis, educators in Paris, and financial managers in Sydney shared the same sentiment. Their gender, age, and education didn't matter. Four out of ten workers were actively thinking about quitting their job sometime in the near future.

THE DATA:

41%

PERCENTAGE OF
GLOBAL EMPLOYEES
CONSIDERING LEAVING
THEIR JOBS

Microsoft Work Index

When Microsoft published the number as part of its Work Trend Index Report, it turned heads. No survey had ever recorded that level of potential change coming in the economy. Could the number be real? Or was it just a snapshot of a workforce in a bad mood, but lacking any real intent to follow through?

Microsoft published its research with this bold observation: "Leaders are out of touch with employees and need a wake-up call."

"Employers Aren't Buying It," declared a headline on CNBC. *Forbes* published an article titled "Why The 'Great Resignation' Is Greatly Exaggerated." *The Business Journal* joined in with an editorial called "Don't Resign Yourself to the Great Resignation."

"It's rational that some people will start looking for new jobs. Will they quit en masse to spite their employers? No, they won't," said *Forbes*.

But a funny thing happened in April 2021. Four million people in the US quit their jobs. The number stunned those who watch the labor markets. No number that high had ever been recorded. Layoffs in one month had hit higher levels during major economic contractions, but the number of voluntary departures from jobs had never been so high. Some thought the number was an aberration. They theorized that all those people who wanted to quit in 2020 but didn't feel the timing was right finally gave their notice in one big push. But then the Bureau of Labor Statistics (BLS) released May's number. Another four million "job quits." And guess what happened in June 2021? Yeah, the number was just as high.

Suddenly, the debate over Klotz's theory faded. He was right. The significant number of resignations was not just a theory. It was now a reality. The auditing powerhouse Deloitte declared that "a seismic shift" was hitting the workforce. A closer look at the data reveals this isn't a three-month trend. Nor is it

THE DATA:

12M

NUMBER OF US EMPLOYEES WHO QUIT THEIR JOBS IN JUST THREE MONTHS

U.S. Bureau of Labor Statistics
(April-June 2021)

a three-year trend. The chart below was published by the Society for Human Resource Management before COVID. It shows the number of US workers who voluntarily left their jobs each year in the last decade. Notice anything? The Great Resignation isn't a theory. It's not something that could happen. It started years ago.

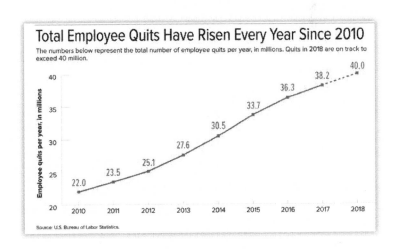

Total Employee Quits Have Risen Every Year Since 2010

The numbers below represent the total number of employee quits per year, in millions. Quits in 2018 are on track to exceed 40 million.

Employee quits per year, in millions

40.0
38.2
36.3
33.7
30.5
27.6
25.1
23.5
22.0

2010 2011 2012 2013 2014 2015 2016 2017 2018

Source: U.S. Bureau of Labor Statistics.

What the lockdown in response to COVID-19 did was pour a massive amount of gasoline on an already-burning fire. It took a tortoise and transformed it into a hare. The number of employees voluntarily leaving companies exploded as the pandemic changed the way we work and altered what people prioritized and tolerated. Perhaps your company started noticing the need for greater employee recruitment and retention a few years ago. Unfortunately, far too few leaders have appreciated the struggle for talent that began worrying HR folks years ago. Many who work in human resources saw the warning signs and knew stronger leadership would be required to interrupt the flow of good people leaving their companies. To make the point, many of them started calling managers "people leaders" and changed their own title to "Chief People Officer." To be honest, even as we flew around the globe trying to convince executives to prioritize culture, we failed to see just how deep the cracks in the foundation really were.

The growing discontent that exists in many workplaces is about so much more than whether people should be allowed to work from home—although we'll dive deep into that in the chapters ahead. In 2021, as the pandemic appeared to be waning, executives announced their Back To Office (BTO) plans. Many of them were totally irritated at all the pushback they got from down the org chart. "Most of us are not hermits," declared one CEO. Another seasoned Fortune 50 HR exec declared working from home "is not going to be sustainable." Another executive openly declared, "I don't see any positives. Not being able to get together in person . . . is a pure negative." And yet another, "We tried it . . . it's just not the same. You just cannot get the same quality of work."

The increased desire for the flexibility to work from home is only one part of a much broader shift only a few careful observers seem to be picking up on. Anyone who steps back and looks at the data and trends walks away seeing something transformative happening. Klotz saw it. And so did a researcher at Deloitte who labeled it "the biggest shift since the Industrial Revolution."

YOUR GREAT-GREAT-GREAT-GRANDFATHER

Seeing the future requires understanding the past. If you go back several generations, you'll discover that your ancestors—like everyone else's—worked on farms. They harvested crops. The world's economy was agricultural. Technology and competition changed that, though. After the Great Depression, farm fields gave way to factories. And suddenly the offspring of farmers joined these things called corporations. Manufacturing corporations. Not everyone worked in factories, but most men did. Radios, cars, televisions, air conditioners, washers and dryers, and refrigerators were all in demand. Two world wars and regional conflicts required even more factories to make weapons and the vehicles to transport them.

Then came the computer. And the next major shift happened. Society flooded into office buildings—and that term actually became inaccurate to describe most of what was inside. "Cubicle building" just doesn't have the same ring to it, though, does it? Buildings full of cubicles popped up everywhere, along with subdivisions, drycleaners, McDonalds, and eventually Starbucks. In 1985, the World Design Conference named the cubicle the most successful design of the previous twenty-five years. And the timing couldn't have been better! Two guys, Steve Jobs and Bill Gates, happened to be working in their separate garages on devices that would fit perfectly into this new workspace.

The shift to the cubicle represented a major shift in what kind of work people were paid for. Farms, factories, mines, and the military largely paid for hard labor. Bodies and hands produced paychecks. But as the workforce shifted to cubicles, companies started paying for people's heads. As a result, technology exploded. The advent of the internet accelerated the speed of idea sharing and reduced the distance from concept to shelf. As walls literally fell and peace largely prevailed for decades, markets expanded at a rate the world had never experienced, and the citizens of the world became connected in a way few had ever imagined possible.

TWO COLLIDING TRENDS

In 1991, Ronald Coase was given a Nobel Prize for something he wrote in 1937 that he called "little more than an undergraduate essay." The boy born in England to two postal workers was a college student when he predicted the rise of something he called "the firm." As he considered the future, he imagined a world dominated by massive corporations.

"The introduction of the firm was due primarily to the existence of marketing costs," Coase wrote. A corporation could afford to promote products and services in a way the entrepreneur never could. Thus, the deep pockets of "firms" would make them incredibly powerful. As he pondered just how large firms might someday become, Coase realized, "A point must be reached where the loss through the waste of resources is equal to the marketing costs." If only he knew how true that would someday become in companies that employ tens of thousands of people.

José Simán @jfsiman · Oct 4, 2020
This was happening before the pandemic and the pandemic just
accelerated the process:

Big Companies Are Starting to **Swallow the World**

Big Companies Are Starting to Swallow the World
The exuberant rebound of large companies while their small
competitors struggle will require more vigilant government antitrust ...
🔗 nytimes.com

Coase was eighty-six years old when fellow Englishman William
Rees-Mogg and American investor James Dale Davidson wrote a
book that hardly anyone read, except every CEO and major investor in Silicon Valley. PayPal's inventor, Peter Theil, said it was the
book that influenced him more than any other. It's a rambling,
intellectual deep dive into history, and a dizzying prophecy of the
future. For our sake, its most important aspect is the title: The
Sovereign Individual. In 1997, ten years after AOL was invented,
and three years after Amazon.com was launched, the book predicted the resurging power of the individual.

The authors claimed the Information Revolution would change
society in a way that would leave no government or economy
untouched.

Just as the printing press ripped power away from the institutional church, the internet would lead to a massive shift of power away from large organizations to the individual.

The Arab Spring, Uber and Upwork, the #MeToo movement, Donald Trump's victory, Brexit, Black Lives Matter, and the term *influencer* were all years away. And yet, when Mark Zuckerberg was twelve years old, Rees-Mogg and Davidson published 416 pages declaring that technology would lead to a resurgence of the individual.

Doug Antin @DougAntin · 13h

Most people are stuck in industries with old rules that resist change.

They live in fear that if they try to implement change, they'll be fired for causing problems.

So they keep their heads down in misery.

That's what makes the ideals of **The Sovereign Individual** so appealing.

"The more widely dispersed key technologies are, the more widely dispersed power will be. The more apparent a system is nearing its end, the more reluctant people will be to adhere to its laws. The Romans were reluctant to acknowledge the changes unfolding around them. So are we," they wrote. "In the future, one of the milestones by which you measure your financial success will be not just how many zeroes you can add to your net worth, but whether you can structure your affairs in a way that enables you to realize full individual autonomy and independence."

Two very different predictions. The rise of the firm. The resurgence of the individual. Could they both be accurate? The data and stories on the pages ahead are evidence of our claim that the collision between these two trends is the shift leaders throughout the world are experiencing. Two different realities crashing into each other, what Deloitte described perfectly as a "seismic" event. This is what you're feeling.

THE PUNCHLINE

 THE DATA:

- 41 percent of global workers said they're considering leaving their job
- 12 million US workers quit their job in just three months as Back to Office plans began rolling out
- The number of employees who have voluntarily left their jobs each year has doubled over the last decade (Pre-COVID)

 THINK ABOUT:

- Workers transitioned from farms to factories to cubicles and now to home offices. When they did, they went from being paid for what they accomplished with their hands to what they come up with in their heads.
- Two trends have been slowly colliding over the last couple of decades:
  - The Rise of the Firm—as predicted by Ronald Coase in his Nobel Prize winning essay called *The Nature of the Firm*. Consolidation has created huge companies in every industry.
  - The Rise of the Individual—as predicted by Rees-Mogg and Davidson in their book, *The Sovereign Individual*. The individual worker has been gaining more power at the same time that the employer has been growing.

WHAT TO DO:

- Acknowledge that there's more movement in the workforce than at any point in your career and it will only get harder to attract and retain the best talent.
- Consider what beliefs exist on your team that could cause someone to leave. Focus on what you control. What experiences can you create to shift those beliefs?
- Acknowledge that as companies get larger, employees feel smaller. What can you do as a leader to make sure your team feels seen and heard?

CHAPTER TWO

THE RISE OF THE INDIVIDUAL

Naval Ravikant is the famous guy most of you have never heard of. Unless you love Twitter and follow visionaries. In the middle of the night on May 31, 2018, Naval did what Donald Trump did far too often and unleashed a tweet storm. Starting at 1:23 a.m. and continuing for nineteen minutes, he sent out forty tweets.

"I thought it was a really crass topic that people would just sort of attack me. I didn't think it would be very popular. But it turns out everyone wants to make money," Naval said days later. More than 160,000 people "liked" the tweets he labeled "How to Get Rich." The tweetstorm landed the angel investor on *The Joe Rogan Experience* and *The Tim Ferriss Show* podcasts, and inspired a follower to publish *The Almanac of Naval Ravikant* on Amazon.

> *"You're not going to get rich renting out your time."*

> *"The Internet has massively broadened the possible space of careers. Most people haven't figured this out yet."*

🐦 *"Don't partner with cynics and pessimists. Their beliefs are self-fulfilling."*

🐦 *"Embrace accountability, and take business risks under your own name. Society will reward you with responsibility, equity, and leverage."*

🐦 *"Labor means people working for you. It's the oldest and most fought-over form of leverage. Labor leverage will impress your parents, but don't waste your life chasing it."*

🐦 *"An army of robots is freely available—it's just packed in data centers for heat and space efficiency. Use it."*

Naval was born in New Delhi and moved to New York with his mom and brother when he was nine. After a brief stint at Boston Consulting Group, he left for Silicon Valley, where he started Epinions.com and later sold it to gain the cash he invested in early rounds of funding for Twitter, Uber, FourSquare, and many others. Those investments and connections led him to found AngelList. Naval is a rare visionary, selling nothing and seemingly unaffected by attention. In a profile by the Wall Street Journal, he said he strives to be "more compassionate, more kind, more honest, and not in it for the short term."

Millions listened and watched as Joe Rogan asked Naval, "I feel like with many people there's this stress accentuated by unhappy lives. By being trapped. There's a big difference not knowing what the meaning of life is and 'God, I got to get the **** out of this job. I can't live my life this way. What's the meaning of life, if this is my life?"

"I was born poor and miserable. Now I'm pretty well-off and happy. There are some principles I've been carrying in my head for thirty years and living them. There are two great addictions: heroin and a monthly salary. You can't get rich renting out your time. We like to view the world as linear. I'm going to put in eight hours of work and get back eight hours of output. It doesn't work that way. The guy running the corner grocery store is working just as hard or harder than you and me. How much output is he getting? What you do, who you do it with, and how you do it are way more important than how hard you work," Naval said.

"It's industrial work with factories that created this current model of thousands of people working together on one thing and having bosses and schedules and times to show up.

I don't care how rich you are. I don't care whether you're a top Wall Street banker. If someone can tell you when to be at work and what to wear and how to behave, you're not a free person. You're not actually rich.

The Information Revolution . . . by making it easier to communicate, connect, and cooperate is allowing us to go back to working for ourselves."

"We are seeing an itemization of the firm. We're seeing the optimal size of the firm shrink. It's most obvious in Silicon Valley. Tons and tons of startups constantly coming up and shaving off little pieces of business of large companies and turning them into huge markets. So what looked like the small little vacation rental market on Craigslist has now suddenly blown up into Airbnb."

"What I think we're going to see is whether it's ten, twenty, fifty, or a hundred years from now, high-quality work will be available. We're not talking about driving an Uber. We're talking about super high-quality work. It will be available in a gig fashion. You'll wake up in the morning. Your phone will buzz. You'll have five different jobs from people who have worked with you in the past or been referred to you. You decide whether to take the project or not. The contract is right there on the spot. You get paid a certain amount and you get rated every day or every week. You get the money delivered and then when you're done working you turn it off and you go to Tahiti or wherever you want to spend the next three months. The smart people have already started figuring out the internet enables this and they're starting to work more and more remotely on their own schedule at their own place with their own friends in their own way. And that's actually how we're the most productive."

Naval struck a nerve. It's the same one Tim Ferriss hit eleven years earlier when he published his first book that instantly made him famous.

"It's too big a world to spend most of life in a cubicle," Ferriss declared in a book called *The 4-Hour Workweek: Escape 9–5, Live Anywhere, And Join the New Rich*. The book argues for people to spend more time on "lifestyle design" than "career planning." "The most fundamental of American questions is hard for me to answer . . . 'So, what do you do?' **I never enjoyed answering this cocktail question, because it reflects an epidemic I was long part of: job descriptions as self-descriptions.**"

For more than a decade, millions of people—some of them your employees—have put in their Airpods and hit the gym listening to books and podcasts by Naval, Ferriss, Gary Vaynerchuk, and others declaring there's a better life than the one they're living. "This idea that we're all factory like cogs in a machine who are specialized and have to do things by rote memorization or instruction is going to go away," Naval said.

And yet to many, it sounded like more like a dream than a real possibility. "Most of you will applaud what I'm saying but you won't actually do it. You have too much fear," Vaynerchuk said on stage more than once. We know he's right. For years, that fear kept us working in Corporate America for bosses we didn't like and wasting more time than we want to admit in meetings and cultures that we wanted out of. We're far from the only ones.

So, what's held people back? What's kept them working for a boss or a company they don't enjoy instead of pursuing the entrepreneurial path that these voices advocate? We know what it was for us, and the data shows it's the same for most people: risk. Humans are wired to survive. We dislike uncertainty more than discomfort. For most people, the risk that comes with leaving a job has kept them in their current one. But five things have shifted in recent years that are profoundly reducing that risk. These factors are making heading for the exit doors much easier.

HIGHER SAVINGS

The Great Recession changed how much money many Americans kept in savings. In 2007 the personal savings rate in the US was below 4 percent. In 2008 it climbed to 6 percent and ultimately averaged above 7 percent for most of the last decade. In 2020 the pandemic sent the number soaring to the highest number on record: 13.7 percent. Keep in mind that number is weighed down by millions of workers who struggle to make it paycheck to paycheck. That means most professionals likely have more in their checking and savings accounts than at any point in their lives. The data shows more people in the workforce saved more money in 2020 and 2021 than in any other years on record.

THE DATA:

💰 **13.7%**

ANNUAL PERSONAL SAVINGS RATE 2020 (HIGHEST ON RECORD IN U.S.)

U.S. Bureau of Economic Analysis

In June 2021 there was more than $4 trillion of personal savings in the US. A year of very little travel, postponed vacations, no high school prom, and kids living at home instead of paying rent at college led to a ton of cash being stashed away. That savings provides safety and security and increases risk tolerance. This, by itself, could be having a huge impact on the level of mobility in the workforce. But wait. This is only the first of five trends leading to the rise of the individual.

Before we move onto the next trend, let's acknowledge that these trends could change at any moment. We've been careful to not cite in this chapter trends that appear to be outliers. Each of the five trends we mention in this chapter have been building over multiple years. The changes brought about by the pandemic accelerated most of these but did not start any of them. Unforeseen events could disrupt any of these trends at any moment, but for now they are influencing the mindset and behavior of many workers, and there's nothing on the horizon currently that would cause us—or the smarter people who study these things more than we do—to believe these things will last just a couple more months.

EXPANDING SOCIAL SAFETY NET

As personal savings have grown, many governments have been expanding their social safety nets. The US government approved more than $1.9 trillion of financial assistance in response to COVID-19. Consider just how much money went to people. $25 billion (not million—we're talking billions here!) was allocated to rent assistance. Ten billion went to mortgage assistance. How many of you who have kids at home were surprised to get a check from the government in July 2021 along with a letter signed by President Biden? People who make hundreds of thousands of dollars a year aren't getting the full $3,600 per child tax credit, but they're getting part of it. Tens of millions of parents are now getting hundreds of dollars a

THE DATA:

🏛 **$1.9T**

TOTAL MONEY IN 'AMERICAN RESCUE ACT' IN RESPONSE TO COVID-19

White House

month per kid. When Russ dropped his daughter off at college in August 2021, he and his wife got home and already had a $500 check in the mail from the university she's attending. They never applied for the money, and it had no letter attached to it, just a note on the check saying it was "COVID-19 tuition relief."

The $1.9 trillion approved by the US government in early 2021 isn't the real story here. What we're focused on is the macro trend. Governments are expanding the social safety net. They're loosening people's dependence on employers and pumping an enormous amount of money into their economies. Americans can go back to the Affordable Care Act (Obamacare) to point to where the trend really began. That act did a lot of things, including making it possible for individuals to log onto Cigna, United, and other health insurance companies' websites and buy their own policies. Add to that the government health exchange, the expanding Health Care Sharing Ministries (HCSM), and health savings accounts, and suddenly people no longer need to work for a large company to have good, affordable health insurance. We were both shocked to learn how many good health coverage options were available to us on our own. Decisions about health care coverage had influenced our employment decisions for most of our lives. That's becoming less and less a factor in choosing where to work. Outside the US this is even less of an issue.

At the time we're writing this book, massive social spending proposals are being debated in Washington D.C. The New York Times described it this way: "Most Americans traditionally have seen the federal government's involvement in their finances once a year, at tax time, when they claim a child credit, get a write-off for the truck they may have bought for their business, or receive a check for an earned income credit, to name a few. That would change profoundly if the social policy bill were enacted. 'If we get this passed, a decade from now, people are going to see many more touch points of government supporting them and their families," Heather Boushey, who sits on President Biden's Council of Economic Advisers, told the Times. Whether a particular bill gets passed or not isn't our concern here. We're giving you context around a trend. Most observers believe regardless of who is elected, the social safety net will continue to expand in most countries.

DEMISE OF NONCOMPETE AGREEMENTS

The rise of the individual is also being fueled by new government regulations. In a move most of you didn't notice, President Biden signed an executive order in the spring of 2021 asking the Federal Trade Commission to take steps to ban—or at a minimum restrict—the use of employee noncompete agreements. In a White House ceremony Biden said he wanted his administration to "curtail the unfair use of noncompete clauses and other clauses or agreements that may unfairly limit worker mobility." Did you hear that? We're not suggesting his action was good or bad. Our opinions don't matter. It's the trend we're more interested in. The current President wants action taken to increase worker mobility. He's not alone. The trend here started at the state level. California, North Dakota, Montana, and Oklahoma already completely ban noncompete agreements in most circumstances. Didn't realize that? Google it! Many other states have restricted the use of noncompete clauses in recent years. Bottom line: employees are gaining more power and "the firm" is losing it.

NPR ✅ @NPR · Jul 9

In an executive order aimed at promoting competition, President Biden is calling on the FTC to ban or limit non-compete agreements that affect tens of millions of U.S. workers.

Biden Moves To Restrict Noncompete Agreements, Saying They're Ba...
In an executive order aimed at promoting competition, President Biden is calling on the Federal Trade Commission to ban or limit noncompete...
𝒮 npr.org

SHRINKING WORK FORCE

For most of your career, the workforce has been growing. It's been driven primarily by two groups: women and minorities. The number of women in the US workforce in 1950 was 18 million. That grew annually all the way to 65 million in 2000. That's an increase of 257 percent over the last fifty years. The Bureau of Labor Statistics expects that growth to only be 40 percent over the next fifty years. At the same time, the number of baby boomers retiring is a much higher number than births to replace them. In 2002 the BLS published a report that predicted, "the high growth rate of the civilian labor force in the last 50 years will be replaced by much lower growth rates in the next 50 years. During the 1950–2000

THE DATA:

📈 **0.5%**

GROWTH RATE OF
THE U.S. WORKFORCE
(WAS 1.6% 1950-2000)

U.S. Bureau of Labor Statistics

period, the annual growth rate was 1.6 percent, whereas, from 2000 to 2050, the annual growth rate is projected to be 0.6 percent." We're halfway through that period, and the rate is actually lower than expected. The labor force is growing at 0.5 percent.

The reality is there are more jobs than people. The trend began before the pandemic. The ratio of workers to job openings dipped to 0.8. In other words, there are 0.8 people to every one job available. After the initial layoffs brought on by the global shutdown in 2020, the ratio again dipped below 1.0. It's why convenience stores and fast-food restaurants started offering something only pro athletes and CEOS used to get: Signing bonuses.

GROWING GIG ECONOMY

These changes all come at the same time that technology is making it increasingly easier to make money without full-time employment. It started in the retail space with sites like E-Bay, Etsy, and the Amazon Marketplace providing a way to sell products to consumers around the globe. Airbnb and VRBO allowed people to rent out their home or spare bedroom. Outdoorsy and RVshare make it possible to make money when you're not using your travel trailer.

Uber, Lyft, Doordash, and Grubhub were more significant developments. Now you could actually make money working when you wanted by simply driving your car around. That expanded to sites where you could hire yourself out as a virtual assistant and now places like Upwork have taken that to a whole new level. Attorneys, accountants, editors, designers, developers, architects, and engineers hire themselves out for gigs rather than work for someone else.

For those who think the gig economy is mainly for young people doing side hustles, you might be surprised to see some of the income levels these folks have made on sites like Upwork. The number is tracked and made public by the site, not the individuals.

Shari is an instructional designer in Maryland who's earned more than $300,000:

Will is a former corporate CFO who has banked more than $400,000 on the site:

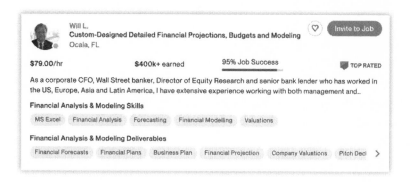

Alex lives in New Jersey and has earned more than $1 million:

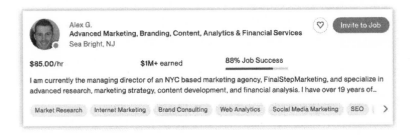

The designer of the cover of this book, the editors who proofread it, and the typesetter who designed each page you're reading are all seasoned professionals we hired online. We've never met any of them. They posted their availability online. We read their reviews—just like you do when you shop on Amazon. We looked at samples of their work. We saw how much money they've made from previous jobs. We sent them direct messages. We interviewed some on Zoom. We sent them a proposal. We hired them and then paid them. Some lived in Europe. Some in South America. Some in the US.

This is the process we used to create this book and our previous books. It's also the process we used to launch our firm. We coach executives around the world without having any employees. Our executive assistants, our bookkeeper, our podcast producer, our social media consultants, our graphic designers, our editors, and our team of coaches of consultants all work for us from wherever in the world they choose to live and get the work done during whatever hours of the day they choose to get stuff done. They have the freedom they desire. And we get world-class talent that are motivated to do a good job so we'll keep using them next month and next year. They love the way they work, and we love paying them only for output and performance.

The Society for Human Resource Management (SHRM) reported in 2020 that "a significant share of the labor force began freelancing for the first time at the onset of the coronavirus pandemic." A study done in October 2020 showed nearly four out of ten people offering services for hire on the internet started doing so after March of 2020.

We're not making this point in an effort to send everyone running to their local HR department to tender their resignation effective immediately! Or to suggest that most people will be joining the Gig Economy in the coming months. We're simply trying to make sure you're aware of the trends. This is our attempt to do our part in providing the "wakeup call" that Microsoft announced in the spring of 2021. These are the headwinds you're up against in trying to attract and retain the best talent.

Rees-Mogg and Davidson were ahead of their time when in 1997 they predicted a trend of increased personal power and control over individual lives.

The signs of that trend are more apparent now than ever. Advances in technology, the expanding social safety net, a decade of increasing rates of personal savings, regulations designed to increase worker mobility, and a workforce that's growing slower than it has in generations, have all combined to create a much more sovereign individual.

THE PUNCHLINE

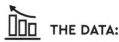 **THE DATA:**

- Five trends are leading to the rise of the individual:

  1. People are saving more money (jumped to 13.7 percent in 2021 but has been steadily climbing since 2009)
  2. Government social safety nets are expanding ($1.9 trillion was approved by the US congress for COVID-19 relief in early 2021.)
  3. Regulations to make it easier for employees to change jobs are expanding (President Biden asked the FTC to make employee noncompete provisions illegal)
  4. The workforce is growing slower than it has in over fifty years (The workforce grew an average of 1.6 percent from 1950 to 2000. The growth has slowed to 0.5 percent in the last twenty years)
  5. The Gig Economy is exploding as the internet decreases dependence on salaries (four out of ten people offering their services online started doing so after March 2020)

 THINK ABOUT:

- Is Naval Ravikant accurate?"There are two great addictions: heroin and a monthly salary. You can't get rich renting out your time."
  - "What you do, who you do it with, and how you do it are way more important than how hard you work."

> o "The smart people have started figuring out the Internet enables this [gig work] and they're starting to work more and more remotely on their own schedule at their own place with their own friends in their own way. And that's actually how we're the most productive."
- If he's right, what does it mean about how you will earn income in five years from now?
- As a leader inside a company, how do you need to adjust in order to attract and retain talent in this environment?

 WHAT TO DO:

- Acknowledge reality. The trends detailed in this chapter will affect your team. They likely already are, but you might not be aware of it. Consider what effect all of this is having on people in your company or on your team.
- Consider what the future of work looks like in your industry. In what ways are you mourning the change rather than adapting to it? What adjustments could you and others make to create a competitive advantage in attracting and retaining talent who want to work differently?

CHAPTER THREE

THE GREAT DISCONTENT

A ll of his top leaders were in the room. More than two hundred people flowed into the huge ballroom just outside Washington DC for a meeting that the Outlook invite called a "Culture Session." These executives were the senior leaders of a hospital system that employed more than fifteen thousand people.

For two hours, small groups rotated around the ballroom writing feedback for each other on large flipcharts. One hospital's leadership team wrote appreciative and constructive feedback on the flipchart for another hospital's leadership team. The finance department, physicians, IT, quality, HR, nursing, and compliance all shared feedback with each other. At the end of two hours, the teams returned to their own flipchart and digested the comments. Some were expected. Others were surprising. The goal was to get these leaders saying what needed to be said to each other.

The CEO of this respected hospital system sat in a tight circle in the corner of the ballroom with his C-suite direct reports and read what others so desperately wanted them to hear. After giving him time with his team, we pulled him aside and prepped him for the closing comments he would make to wrap up the meeting. We coached him to consider thanking the group for their candor and create an experience that caused the people in the room to feel his level of ownership of what he had heard.

A few minutes later, the seasoned executive stood in the front of the room and spoke humbly and forcefully into the microphone in his hand. "**I have come to an inconvenient and disgusting truth. I am the problem**," he said slowly. We were so shocked by what he said we didn't hear much of the rest. We've been in meetings like this more than a few times, and we've never heard a leader internalize feedback so dramatically. There was no anger or defensiveness in his voice. He seemed completely disappointed and deflated. Honestly, we felt like giving him a hug. We instead thanked him for his genuineness and reminded him of our call the following week to debrief and plan next steps. With that, we darted for Reagan National Airport. That phone call with the CEO never happened. In fact, we never talked with him or saw him again because he resigned.

Days after that meeting, this man who had helped build this regional hospital system into a dominant force in the market submitted his resignation to the board. The board had demanded action months earlier following a dismal employee engagement survey. Scores weren't bad at one hospital or in one department. They were terrible across the system. Our phone rang when the executive team decided action was needed to demonstrate they were addressing the problem. Their survival depended on taking important steps to fix a toxic culture. We were in the beginning stages of that process when the CEO left. And then the COO. Then the Chief

Nursing Officer and the Chief Medical Officer. Eventually every member of that team was gone. These were all great people with tons of wisdom and experience. They were respected in the hospital industry. Their system was revered by healthcare systems across the country for their incredible financial results. By most metrics they were best of class. Except one. And it ended up being the metric that matters most.

As the individual has gained more power in the workplace, two things have happened. One has been building for a while. The other is new and was brought on by the pandemic. Employees are experiencing discontent and their priorities have shifted. Let's dig into both these drivers of The Great Resignation to better understand what's really happening.

THE DATA:

1. DISCONTENT
2. SHIFT IN PRIORITIES

REASONS PEOPLE ARE QUITTING JOBS

Microsoft Work Index & Gallup

THE GREAT DISCONTENT

Shortly after Professor Klotz coined the phrase "The Great Resignation," the Gallup organization published an article with the title, "The Great Resignation is Actually the Great Discontent." Their research showed 48 percent of people across all job categories were actively looking for a new job. Why? "It's a workplace issue," Gallup announced.

This issue isn't new. Gallup started measuring employee engagement more than two decades ago. They were the first vendor to sell leaders a survey that claimed to reveal how much their employees like their jobs. Dozens of competitors and pulse survey providers have sprung up over the years. Remarkably, they all show the exact same problem. Google the question "how many employees are disengaged?" You'll get the same response to that search today as you would have ten years ago. The answer is seven out of ten employees aren't happy. The trend hasn't changed one bit the entire time Gallup and similar companies have been measuring employee satisfaction.

Think of that for a moment.

Seven out of ten employees are disengaged and have been for two decades. Why is no one—or almost no one—making progress on this problem?

We have a theory. If a company is hitting its revenue numbers, meeting its goals for quality, hitting safety metrics, and keeping the customer coming back for more why would employee engagement really matter? It hasn't. Until now. Or actually, about five years ago.

That's when we started to see more and more companies replace Employee Engagement as a Key Result with Employee Retention.

As the economy strengthened between 2015 and 2020 and unemployment trended downward, disengaged employees started doing something they hadn't done before. They quit. Why tolerate a toxic culture when other companies are hiring? The trend has been accelerated not only by historically low unemployment, but also by the growth of the firm.

Multiple studies show the larger the company, the lower the employee engagement. Obviously, there are exceptions. But that's the rule. In small companies, employees are closer to leaders who can make a difference in the direction of the company. They feel heard and feel greater transparency.

"Employees who work for larger companies with more than 1,000 workers report lower levels of engagement than those who work for smaller firms with fewer than 1,000 employees. The engagement gap widens for employees who work for companies with more than 5,000 workers, as these individuals report lower average results on nearly all of Gallup's engagement items than in firms with fewer than 1,000 employees." Gallup reported. As consolidation accelerates across all industries, organizations get bigger and often employees feel increasingly invisible. Their engagement depends heavily on whether they feel seen and heard. That doesn't happen without intentional effort by leaders. All too often, those leaders don't know how to do that. They've never been trained on managing culture or how to improve employee satisfaction. Instead, they're tasked with coming up with an action plan to increase their engagement scores and left to figure it out on their own.

THEIR PRIORITIES HAVE CHANGED!

When the pandemic caused everyone to spend more time at home, something transformative happened for most of us. We heard it on a call with members of our team when one of our colleagues who crisscrossed the globe as much as we did pre-COVID said, "for the first time since my kids were born, I'm actually coaching one of their soccer teams. I will never go back to traveling that much again." We felt the same way. Russ drove the neighborhood carpool for the first time in his life, and Jared made it to every one of his daughter's high school soccer games.

In Microsoft's head-turning study that signaled The Great Resignation was about to begin, researchers highlighted a shift in priorities happening across the global workforce. "With so much change upending people over the past year, employees are reevaluating priorities, home bases—their entire lives. Whether due to fewer networking or career advancement opportunities, a new calling, pent up demand, or a host of pandemic-related struggles, more and more people are planning a change," the report said.

Perhaps it was becoming more aware of our own mortality. Or maybe it was being deeply impacted by protests demanding greater equality in cities across the world. For some it might have been interacting with our kids more rather than sending them to daycare. Others might have decided life is too short to work for a toxic boss. **Or maybe the increased volume of emails and Zoom meetings during the pandemic caused us to question whether this is the life we really wanted**. Whatever the specific cause, the data shows millions of workers have changed their priorities after the experiences of 2020 and 2021.

Britt Altizer put in long hours as a restaurant manager until the pandemic temporarily shut the place down. Britt was suddenly furloughed and wondering how to pay the bills for his small family. "I did some soul searching. During the time I was home, I was gardening and really loving life," Britt told Time Magazine. "I realized working outdoors was something I had to get back to doing." At the same time, his wife, Kari, quit her job in the insurance industry to spend more time at home helping to take care of their infant son just as the pandemic was beginning. She said the time at home changed her perspective. "We aren't supposed to live to work. We're supposed to work to live," she said. She decided to help her husband start a landscaping company so he can be outdoors and they can spend more time together.

"Before the pandemic, Americans spent 5 percent of their working time at home," *The Economist* magazine reported. "By the spring of 2020 the figure was 60 percent. The shift has gone better than expected."

Changing priorities caused employees to reevaluate what they do for a living, who they work for, who they work alongside, the mission and purpose of their company, and how it all fits into their long-term plans. We're fairly confident that in the recent past, you've spent some time considering these things. We all have. For millions of people, it's already led to changes in where they work. That trend will continue.

THE DATA:

🏠 66%

PEOPLE WHO SAY THEY'RE MORE EFFECTIVE WORKING FROM HOME

Linkedin's Workforce
Confidence Data

HOW LEADERS SHOULD RESPOND

In the middle of writing this chapter, we were on a call with a client. She works for a Fortune 10 company. At the beginning of the call, she informed us she was about to submit her resignation. She said she couldn't tolerate the culture anymore. Her voice had been ignored far too often, she told us. Within days of starting to look for something else, she had an attractive offer. She accepted. Her departure was universally viewed as a setback by her team and the executives who worked alongside her.

How do we prevent that kind of scenario from playing out on our team? Some turnover is natural and positive at every organization, but we want to keep most of our best people with us as long as possible. The second half of this book is all about solutions to the challenges identified in the first half. So we'll dig into what's working regarding attracting and retaining the best talent in this new environment. But we want to offer you some warning signs to look for when your employees start signaling that they don't feel as engaged or wonder if this job fits into their new order of priorities.

THE DISENGAGEMENT CYCLE®

When employees become disengaged or start wondering if their job is really a good fit for them, they tend to send signals as a warning. This doesn't happen every time with everyone, but it's consistent enough to be considered the norm. We've seen this cycle play out in our years of being hired to help leaders increase engagement and help shift their culture.

Employees rarely leave their jobs without first warning people they are frustrated. The challenge is that most leaders aren't actively watching for these warning signs.

Make Noise

The first signal we send when becoming disengaged is making noise. In this stage, we speak up directly or tell others our concerns. We raise our hand or work with others to get our point of view into the light of day. We do whatever we can to get our leader's attention. We have something of value to contribute or something they're overlooking that's critical to consider. How others respond to our concerns or opinions matters tremendously. We want to work for leaders and companies that value what's in our head as much as what we contribute with our hands. Leaders who seek their team's feedback and genuinely listen to others have more engaged teams. When we attach lots of emotion to our opinion or perspective, it's usually a sign we're deep in the Make Noise stage. We're desperately trying to find someone who will listen to our concerns. The longer we feel undervalued, the more likely we'll start to speak up in a way perceived by others as negative, cynical, critical, or sarcastic. Our efforts to be heard are no longer viewed as productive or helpful.

Blame Others

When making noise doesn't seem to work, we tend to slip deeper into disengagement. We enter the Blame Others stage. We want empathy. We're seeking an audience anywhere. We want someone to validate our perspective or to acknowledge the obstacles we're trying to overcome. We tend to find the most receptive audience with others who are at the same level of disengagement, who have had similar experiences with leaders in the company and are equally or more frustrated. These conversations are almost never productive. We feel heard emotionally, but those listening to us are rarely those who can do anything about our frustrations. Venting feels good momentarily, but to others it sounds like we're playing the blame game. Much of the time, we don't realize we're in this stage.

Go Silent

The biggest warning sign of a culture that's become toxic is silence. When we enter a room—physical or virtual—nothing is more concerning more than a team that's not talking. In Zoom or Microsoft Teams, that looks like cameras off and mics muted. In an on-site meeting, it's lack of eye contact, hands in laps, and hesitation to offer opinions. We enter the 'go silent' stage after we've tried speaking up but no one seemed to listen. We've spent time and energy venting to others but that hasn't changed anything. Eventually, we just withdraw. We clock in and we clock out. We log in but stay silent. The leader has proven again and again he or she isn't interested in listening.

Disengaged employees tend to cycle through these various stages. They might decide to speak up in a particular meeting or conversation after spending months being silent. If their opinion is once again not considered, they typically revert back and continue the cycle. After several attempts to feel valued and enough cycles through these three stages, most employees begin planning their exit.

When people are sending these signals or sinking deeper into any of these three stages, it requires leadership to reengage those individuals. These are the early indicators of a looming retention problem. **Too often managers wait for employee engagement surveys to tell them if their teams are engaged or not. There's no need to wait for a survey**. Don't ignore the signs. In this new environment, these signals equal employee retention problems. Your best people won't tolerate being ignored, sidelined, or silenced.

THE PUNCHLINE

 THE DATA:

- Gallup said 48 percent of employees are actively looking for a new job. The biggest reason? Discontent.
- Seven out of ten employees have been disengaged in their jobs. That average has been consistent for more than 20 years. The current approach isn't working.
- Employee disengagement started to lead to employee departures in 2010. As unemployment dipped and the economy heated up, the number of employees quitting their jobs doubled in the last decade. The pandemic poured gasoline on an already-burning fire.

THINK ABOUT:

- As employees have gained greater mobility due to the trends detailed in Chapter 2, they have also felt more discontent.
- The discontent is due to two factors:
  - The culture that exists on their team. Too many employees don't feel heard or seen.
  - People's priorities have shifted. Sending more than half the workforce home for an extended period changed their perspective about what's most important.

- Surveys can measure the level of discontent but there's a much more efficient way for leaders to know if their employees are becoming disengaged.
  - The Disengagement Cycle® shows that when employees experience discontent they:
    - Make Noise
    - Blame Others
    - Go Silent
  - Leaders looking for these warning signs can respond quickly and retain top talent.

 **WHAT TO DO:**

- Acknowledge reality. Consider what beliefs your employees hold that are causing them to feel discontent. What experiences are creating that discontent? Focus on what you can control and start creating experiences that shift those beliefs.
- Consider which of your employees in any of the phases of The Disengagement Cycle®. How can you help them feel heard?
- Consider whether you are demonstrating behavior in any of the three phases of The Disengagement Cycle®. If you are, who should you talk to and what could you do to become fully engaged?
- If that doesn't work, what decisions do you need to make to improve your well-being? Focus on what you control.

CHAPTER FOUR

PROCESS AND PEOPLE

t's the magazine that carries more weight than any other among Fortune 500 executives. In July 2015 the *Harvard Business Review* put a bomb on its cover and boldly proclaimed, "It's time to blow up HR."

If you opened the glossy publication and flipped to the cover story, the headline read "People Before Strategy." "Managing human capital must be accorded the same priority that managing financial capital came to have in the 1980s, when the era of the 'super CFO' and serious competitive restruc-

turing began," the magazine said. The article advocated major changes at the C-suite level. We'll get more into that in a moment, but this is about far more than HR. This is about how leaders at every level of every organization view their role. Is their job to develop and execute a strategy? Or is it to manage the environment or culture? The editors at Harvard were making their case that people management clearly wasn't a high enough priority in most companies.

LOSING PEOPLE AT THE PLANT

About ten months into the COVID-19 pandemic, we got a call from the CEO of a manufacturing company. He was months away from opening a big new plant in North America that would more than double his production capability in the US. As construction moved forward, he had a problem at his existing plant. An employee engagement survey exposed that people weren't happy. Plant managers blamed their worsening employee retention numbers on COVID, but the survey made the CEO wonder if his problem was less about the pandemic than about the leadership of the facility. He asked us to travel to the plant and see what we uncovered.

We interviewed dozens of people, including the plant leadership team, as well as new and veteran production line employees. Almost everyone complained about the newly implemented, temporary six-day workweek. "I have a little girl and the only time I really get to spend time with her is on the weekends," one woman wearing the plant uniform of dark pants, a button up long-sleeve shirt, steel-toed boots, a baseball cap, and mask told us. "They don't seem to care how the Saturdays affect my family," she said referring to her bosses.

A few hours after she made that comment, an executive stood in the front of a training room reviewing PowerPoint slides detailing the plant's performance. The number of units coming off the line was on-target. The quality scores of the product were exceptional. Safety goals were being met. Demand for the product was huge, with a whopping $500 million backlog. Chart after chart showed just how well things were going at the plant. Then the executive got to the last slide. It showed employee retention. People were quitting faster than they could be replaced.

How could a plant that was meeting or exceeding every measure of success be losing people so fast?

The leaders were masters of process, but rookies in people management.

They were spending all of their time tracking product and talking about procedures and hardly any time building relationships with and developing their people. Given the flattening of the labor pool, how sustainable do you think those results will be if they can't keep the people who know how to deliver them?

THE DATA:

 12%

PERCENTAGE OF LEADERS WHO SAY THEY KNOW HOW TO MANAGE ENGAGEMENT & CULTURE

Deloitte Human Capital Trends Report

The head of the plant was a kind, soft-spoken man who had spent decades mastering manufacturing. He spent almost every hour sitting in his office near the entrance of the plant or in meetings with corporate executives. His team did what all leadership teams do and followed his lead. Those with offices or cubicles lived in them. Lower-level supervisors who monitored the production line rarely spoke up except when they saw mistakes. "They don't even know me," said one line worker in our interview. "You know more about my family than any of them do, and you just met me," he said.

Leaders have two levers they can pull to deliver results: strategy and culture. Process and people. As Ronald Coase's prediction has come true and the average firm has gotten larger, most organizations have put all their energy into strategy. Leaders know culture is important but have no idea how to define it or manage it.

LEAVING HARVARD FOR UBER

Frances Frei was teaching at the Harvard Business School when she got the call. Uber needed her. The ride-sharing company wasn't looking for another driver. They needed someone to fix their people problem. The company was on a meteoric rise when an internal crisis threatened its future. Allegations of sexual harassment, discrimination, and bullying involving multiple executives including the CEO started making headlines. One news outlet said the company had "Silicon Valley's most obvious version of toxic culture." The New York Times said Uber had "become a prime example of Silicon Valley start-up culture gone awry."

Frei took a sabbatical from her "dream job" at Harvard and moved out west to take on the challenge of helping fix Uber. She told us the first thing she noticed after being named SVP of leadership was "they didn't know what the levers were for building and losing trust, because no one would deliberately lose as much as they had." As the company's employee count soared, all the attention had been placed on an aggressive growth strategy with no attention given to people management. "Many, many people were put in the position of manager. And it was almost a faith-based position. It was as if I put you there somehow you'll learn it. **If you want to be an effective leader, the first thing to understand is it's about others. We need to be taught how to be leaders of others**," Dr. Frei told us.

What Frei discovered at Uber was that a few bad apples were creating most of the problems. Once they were moved out, and a leadership development program was created to upskill leaders on people management, it didn't take long for the culture to move from toxic to healthy. After helping Uber get back on track, Frances returned to Harvard where she lobbied to move culture to the first-year curriculum at the business school. People management needed to be taught to students at the beginning of the study of how to lead organizations.

GOOGLE AND CHICK-FIL-A

Google's longtime head of human resources, Laszlo Bock, used to get tons of things in the mail from people who desperately wanted to work for the tech giant. "I post the more colorful ones on my wall, including one letter than included the phrase 'culture eats strategy for breakfast.' I'd never heard that phrase but thought it silly enough to keep as an example of management gibberish," Bock wrote in his memoir of his time at Google.

"To my astonishment, that phrase was pretty spot-on. I realized this only after I'd been at Google five years. Our culture was shaping our strategy, and not the other way around. It took me another few years to wonder where the phrase came from. I learned it was . . . attributed to the influential management theorist Peter Drucker. It hangs on the wall of the Ford Motor Company's war room, posted there in 2006 by Ford's president, Mark Fields, as a reminder that a robust culture is essential to success."

Jimmy Collins helped build Chick-fil-A from its original spot as a neighbor of Hog Dog on a Stick in suburban mall food courts in the 1980s to the indisputable powerhouse in standalone fast-food restaurants. Collins was Chick-fil-A's president for decades. From his home in suburban Atlanta, Jimmy told us a story of how he managed culture at a company that's universally recognized as being among the best at it in any industry.

"I went into a store one day. I could go into any store outside Atlanta and they wouldn't know me. I liked to order my food, go to the table, and take a look at it. One day I opened the bag and looked in there. There were my waffle fries. I thought, oh gosh, I gotta go to the kitchen. So I went into the kitchen. I scared them all to death. I asked who made my waffle fries. This young man said, 'I did.' I said I want everybody in the kitchen to come over here. I said I want to show you what this young man did to my waffle fries. I showed them the bag. I said 'what do you all think of these?' I showed them a bag full of fries. I said, 'that's the way the customer likes them. This makes them feel like they're getting their money's worth when the bag's full."

"Then I dumped them out on the counter. I picked one up. I said, 'Look at that. Just look at it. It's golden brown. I had them all put their hands on those fries. Then I picked one up and put it in my mouth. It made a lot of noise as I crunched down on it. Just the perfect crunch."

"I said to that group in the kitchen, 'if this young man keeps making waffle fries, our customers are not going to be able to wait to get back in here. This young man is an expert. Just come here every day and make waffle fries like that, okay,'"

"To manage people you have to change from being a critic to be an encourager. I don't want to be the critic. I've worked on that. I'm still working on it today," the retired Collins told us.

HOW TO MANAGE PEOPLE

Three deaths in one year. Each of the victims was under thirty years of age. All of them would have survived if they had worn their safety harness.

It was shortly after the third death that we found ourselves sitting in the office of the CEO. This leader was anxious to describe his company's commitment to safety. He rattled off a bunch of policies and procedures that should have prevented the accidents. He talked about all the safety training meetings that were held on a regular basis. This utility company prided itself on its commitment to safety, and this seasoned executive was laying out the evidence.

As our team dug deeper into that company's culture in the weeks after that meeting, we discovered something. The oldest and most experienced employees seemed to disregard the safety policies. They were the worst offenders when it came to not wearing protective gear. Yes, they had attended all the training meetings and knew the policies, but they disregarded them. Why? Well, because they had been doing this job for years and knew how to avoid the dangers of working on utility lines. They weren't wrong. The data did show the experienced employees weren't the ones who had been involved in any of the accidents.

What our team discovered, though, was that the veterans were the problem. Here's why: guess who the younger and less experienced employees were watching? Right! They were taking cues from the older teammates who went to the safety training meetings but disregarded the instructions. The newer crew members held a belief. They believed that safety harnesses weren't actually needed and that all the policies and procedures were a waste. Not only that, but they believed that the more seasoned technicians looked down on them for following all the rules.

We pulled some of the older techs together and told them "You're killing these kids." They were shocked. They hadn't considered the impact of their unwillingness to wear the harness. One of the techs actually teared up. We asked them what beliefs they wanted the new team members to hold about safety and what experiences were they willing to create to ensure no one was ever hurt on the job. In that moment, the mindset of the more experienced team members shifted. They realized they were part of the problem. The change in the culture was palpable. Every crew member started wearing the harness every time. No exceptions! Many of them weren't wearing it because they thought they needed it, but because they wanted the newer team members to be protected.

The mindset of a team is largely a result of the experiences created by leaders. The mindset and culture, so clearly detectable to customers of Chick-fil-A, didn't happen by accident. Every time Jimmy went into a restaurant and created an experience like he described with those waffle fries, he was managing the culture. What are the chances the owner of that location called his friends who owned other franchises and told them that story? The higher on the org chart someone is, the bigger the wake formed by the experiences they create. All too often, leaders think of their job as managing processes rather than leading people.

Any leader can deliver short-term results, but in order to sustain and scale results, you have to build a team that has clarity and alignment. Alignment, trust, collaboration, and candid communication are signs of a healthy organization.

One of the positive signs over the last five years is an increasing number of organizations elevating some sort of people-management metric into their set of most important results. It's not uncommon now for a financial metric, a customer-satisfaction number, and an employee-retention or employee-satisfaction metric to make up an organization's Key Results. As the number of resignations increased over the last several years, leaders started tracking retention and engagement. They eliminated the Chief Human Resources Officer role and created the Chief People Officer or Chief Talent Officer position and started talking more about leadership development.

The challenge is the effort has stalled.

Companies are tracking employee retention and engagement, but most executives aren't sure how to respond to subpar metrics in those categories. Organizations are still far more reactionary than proactive when it comes to people management.

When engagement scores dip, executives review the charts of survey results with managers, but then task them with creating an "action plan" to address the discontent. Managers do their best to come up with something that looks good on paper and then usually get lost in the fire of the moment the next week. No one follows up and employees see no change in how they're being managed. The cycle repeats itself and discontent continues to grow.

The key to people management is to consider the beliefs you need your team to hold, and then create experiences designed to foster those beliefs. In the second half of this book, we'll review with you what the data and our experience coaching and consulting with leaders show are the most important beliefs you need your team to hold in order to attract and retain talent in the work environment of the next three to five years.

Leaders who do the following will drive engagement, lower the level of discontent, increase employee retention, and create an environment that accelerates business outcomes:

- Demonstrate flexibility
- Obsess over the customer
- Validate diversity
- Collaborate selectively
- Prioritize and focus

In the chapters that follow we'll review the data and make the case that these five areas deserve the most attention to minimize the impact your team and company feel from The Great Resignation.

THE PUNCHLINE

 THE DATA:

- Only 12 percent of leaders say they know how to effectively manage culture and employee engagement.
- As individual workers gain more power and mobility while simultaneously experiencing discontent themselves (Chapters 2 and 3), most leaders struggle with what to do. They feel underdeveloped in effective people management. Most companies don't have a people management strategy or plan designed to help those team leaders attract and retain the best people.
- People management comes down to managing experiences and beliefs.

 **THINK ABOUT:**

- What aspects of your company's culture attracted your best people to work there?
- Has any of that changed in the last one to two years?
- What impact is it having?
- What are two or three ways your team needs to think and act differently to be engaged and deliver the necessary results?

 **WHAT TO DO:**

- Acknowledge reality. Consider getting the perspectives of some members of your team on the questions above.
- Consider two or three beliefs you need your team to hold in order to accelerate achieving the results you've got to deliver.
- Consider one or two experiences you could create in the next week that would start driving those beliefs.
- Focus on what you control. Take accountability for the mindset on your team. Acknowledge the experiences created by the leaders you report to (good or bad) but don't become preoccupied by it. Shape the narrative for those who report to you.

PART TWO

HOW LEADERS
MUST ADAPT

CHAPTER FIVE

DEMONSTRATE FLEXIBLILITY

"**W**here is he? Why isn't he here yet?" Russ's boss wanted to know why "Jason" wasn't in his office. This was years ago. Jason was one of Russ's best salespeople. He crushed his numbers. Clients loved him. No one generated more new business and took care of existing clients better than Jason. And yet he drove the CEO of the company crazy. He couldn't stand that Jason never showed up at work when everyone else did. The company had a strict eight to five work schedule that everyone was expected to comply with. Tardiness was not tolerated.

"His office door is locked and no one's seen him yet," the CEO said to Russ.

"I'm not worried about it. He was probably in Houston last night and got home late. He'll be in today. It's not something we need to concern ourselves with," Russ said to his boss. To Russ, what mattered most were results. Jason was delivering. He always delivered. As long as he was hitting his number, why should anyone care whether he was sitting at his desk in his office?

Russ's boss saw it differently. He cared deeply about the activities of the employee. His concern was whether Jason was wasting precious time during the day that could have driven even higher sales numbers.

The important question is what matters most? Activity or results? Which one do you want to create accountability for on your team?

When most of the workforce was suddenly sent home due to the pandemic, many leaders worried about not being able to see or track what their employees were doing. "We tried it . . . it's just not the same. You just cannot get the same quality of work," Rajat Bhageria, the CEO of Chef Robotics, told the Wall Street Journal. JPMorgan Chase & Co.'s Jamie Dimon said at a conference in 2021 that working remotely doesn't work "for those who want to hustle."

THE DATA:

🏠 **20%**

PERCENTAGE WHO WORKED AT HOME SOME PORTION OF THEIR WEEK PRE-2020

🏠 **71%**

PERCENTAGE WHO WORKED AT HOME AT SOME POINT DURING 2020

PEW Research Center

The CEO of Rite Aid saw it very differently. Heyward Donigan told the WSJ, "We have adapted to work-from-home unbelievably well. I had a philosophy that I want to hire the best and the brightest even if they work from a different location, and now, ironically, we're all working from another location. We've learned that we can work remote, and we can now hire and manage a company remotely."

Two very different perspectives on the same situation. One sees their company thriving as everyone works in a whole new way. Another views anything different than the way it used to be as a disaster. Some companies have declared their employees never have to return to the office. Some have gone to a structured hybrid approach where people are expected in the office on certain days. Others are allowing employees and teams to determine what works best for them. And others want everyone back every day just like it was pre-COVID.

While executives debate what the future should look like, the data is absolutely clear on what employees want.

The research overwhelmingly shows employees want flexibility more than anything in how they work moving forward. The word has come up over and over again in survey after survey. If the pandemic taught workers across the globe a common lesson it was this: the way we used to work isn't the way we have to work moving forward. Work can get done at home. Employees don't have to be in the office every day. Virtual meetings can be very effective in the right circumstances.

THE DATA:

↻ **83%**

PERCENTAGE OF EMPLOYEES
WHO WANT A HYBRID
WORK MODEL

Accenture Research

To some, the pandemic exposed how much work had become like adult daycare. Everyone is expected to be in at a certain time. They're expected to stay till a certain time. And it's best to look busy in between.

Every job in every department in every company required the same basic number of hours a week: forty. Or more. When you step back and consider the model of how most of us worked before COVID-19, it can start to look pretty ridiculous. This is what Naval Ravikant has been saying for years that is now finally getting a lot of attention.

"It's industrial work with factories that created this current model of thousands of people working together on one thing and having bosses and schedules and times to show up. I don't care how rich you are. I don't care whether you're a top Wall Street banker. If someone can tell you when to be at work and what to wear and how to behave you're not a free person," Ravikant said.

Right after graduating from college, Jared took a full-time marketing job at a small newspaper. Within a few weeks, he realized he could finish the tasks described by his boss in about twenty hours. So what to do with the remaining 50 percent of his time? He brought several proposals forward suggesting ways to drive the business, but was told, "We just need you to do the things on the list. If you get them done, just stick around for the rest of the time." Wow! That's a pretty extreme example, but many companies are doing the same thing today.

Sure, there are some industries and workplaces that demand set schedules and people on location. But many of us have teams that don't work on factory floors, serve food, or unlock dressing rooms. **If you're hiring and paying people for what's in their head, why are you treating them the same as someone who is paid for what they do with their hands? It's no wonder so many employees feel discontent.** Russ once had an executive assistant who was a former nun. She was deeply religious and had a magnet on the filing cabinet behind her desk that read, "Jesus is coming. Look busy!" The magnet made Russ chuckle every time he saw it. Isn't that the attitude of many bosses? We want our people where we can see them every hour of every day and we want them to look busy.

When you demand accountability for activity, you get lots of activity. When you create accountability for results, you accelerate achievement of results. People will always find time to fill their schedules. They will find ways to stay busy. That doesn't mean they're doing the things that matter most.

Please introduce us to the shareholder that values activity. Show us the board member that hands out trophies for being busy. One of the most significant shifts a leader can help their team make is understanding they're paid to deliver results. Far too many leaders are obsessed with activity. For those leaders, nothing is more uncomfortable than not being able to see Jason in his office at 8 a.m. every day.

THE FUTURE IS HYBRID

The question is no longer whether the future of work will be hybrid, but rather what that hybrid environment will look like. A senior executive of a large company sent us a message asking if we would jump on a call to review their back-to-office plan. "There's a lot of collaboration that happens when people work alongside each other physically. We want to be flexible but we also need to make sure these teams and departments are interacting with each other," he told us. We asked what that looked like.

"We're planning to have people come into the office three days a week," he said. We asked if the employees got to determine what three days they came in or if it would be dictated by their bosses. "We can't have some people here some days and others here other days. That doesn't solve our need for greater collaboration," he told us. "So, we're thinking everyone has to be here Monday, Tuesday, and Wednesday. They can decide whether to work from home or come in the end of the week."

We probed a little deeper. "How long do people need to be at the office on those days? Is there a certain time they need to show up? Do they have to stay until a certain time? What if they want to go to the gym at 9 a.m.? Can you leave to go coach a kid's soccer or dance team? What if they show up and have no meetings with other teams two days during the week and no cross-functional meetings are scheduled, and they don't experience any collaboration on most days? How does your Back to Office plan address all of those questions?" we asked.

He sighed. "I'm not sure how we feel about all of that," he said.

Your employees have experienced months or even more than a year of no rush-hour traffic. They've shifted their workouts away from 4:30 a.m. They've picked up the kids after school. They've taken mom to lunch and done a little shopping during the workday. They've gotten used to calling into some meetings while doing laundry or driving to the store. In other words, they've experienced flexibility. And the data shows they never want to lose it again.

Our call with the executive seeking feedback on the company's Back to Office plan ended with us asking, "Do your employees know what results they need to deliver? Do you trust them to come up with a plan of how they can best deliver those results?" Flexibility is a sign of trust. It's an acknowledgment that you consider your employees adults. It's evidence that you truly believe you have hired qualified and competent people.

THE DATA:

32%

PERCENTAGE OF EXECUTIVES WHO SAID CULTURE WAS THEIR TOP CONCERN IN THE NEW WORKPLACE. THEIR NEXT HIGHEST CONCERN WAS PRODUCTIVITY FOLLOWED BY COLLABORATION.

Deloitte Return to Workplace Survey

Some of your employees value connection more than anything else. They desperately want to be in the office most of the week. Others value freedom and independence the most. They want to be home more than they're at the office. Both groups want flexibility to determine what works best for them.

THE CORE OF FLEXIBILITY IS AGILITY

We're spending a decent amount of ink talking about flexibility as it relates to where your team works. But, that's far from the only area that employees want flexibility in. They want more trust and empowerment in all areas of their jobs. We've tried to make this point repeatedly in this book by explaining the transition from farms to factories and then to cubicles and how far too many leaders are still treating employees as if they worked in a factory.

The challenge we're up against in trying to make this case is that most of you think you're dang good at being flexible. You pride yourself on it. And yet the reality is you're not. Or at least your team thinks you're not. We know this from spending most of the last two decades helping companies dig into the shifts needed in their culture. Until now, most people haven't used the word flexibility.

Employees say they want greater trust and empowerment from those up the org chart. Executives say they want greater agility and challenging of the status quo down the org chart. Doesn't this all come down to the same thing?

Employees want flexibility to do things the way they think is best and their bosses want their teams to be willing to do things differently than in the past. One of our favorite books of 2021 was *Think Again* by Adam Grant. In that book, Grant challenges all of us to be willing to be more agile and pliable in how we view things. He says most people—most of us—often resist being flexible by saying things like:

- That will never work here
- That's not what my experience has shown
- That's too complicated, let's not overthink it
- That's the way we've always done it

Mark Twain famously said, "It ain't what you know that gets you into trouble. It's what you know for sure that just ain't so."

THE AGILITY INDEX®

As our clients have asked us to help their organizations become more flexible or agile, we've been asked to consider what that looks like. What questions would help someone know if they're agile? How would we know if one person is more agile than another? Working with our coaching and consulting clients we developed three questions called The Agility Index®.

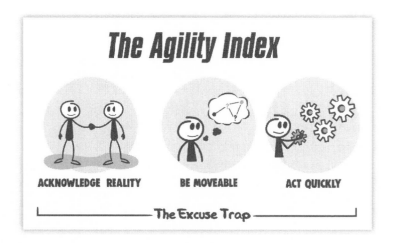

ACKNOWLEDGE REALITY

The first question to consider in assessing your flexibility or agility as a leader is to ask yourself:

How willing am I to acknowledge reality?

We encourage you to answer that question by rating yourself 1 to 10. Giving yourself a 1 means your head is firmly in the sand and your mind is in complete denial of how things really are. A 10 means you're not attached to any particular narrative or thinking of how things should be. You see things for how they really are with no thought of how that reality might affect you.

One of our clients manufactures IV bags, lots of them! Just before the pandemic, there was a significant IV bag shortage. The three largest suppliers were all behind in their manufacturing. Hurricane Maria hit Puerto Rico hard in 2017, and some of the largest IV manufacturing facilities for the Unites States are there. Power was knocked out, facilities were offline, workers were in survival mode and fresh water was a major concern. This was an epic disaster for everyone in Puerto Rico, and the last thing they were worried about was getting back to work.

But when you're a cancer patient who needs your life saving therapy, you don't want to hear about IV bag shortages. You want to hear the solution to the problem!

Doctors and nurses couldn't simply ignore the fact that IV bags were in short supply; they had to get creative and come up with new ways to care for patients. They had to acknowledge the reality that there wouldn't be enough IV bags anytime soon and that they had to come up with a different approach. New procedures were developed to deliver medication in ways that didn't require IVs. One approach was to use syringe pumps where saline solution was mixed with medication in the tube of the syringe and delivered directly to the patient by a nurse. It took longer, but it worked.

THE DATA:

🦻 **73%**

EMPLOYEES WHO SAY THEIR COMPANY STRUGGLES TO HEAR THE HARD THINGS.

Workplace Accountability Study

John Willis, the CEO of a global tech firm, was listening intently as we reported findings from a round of interviews we conducted with his leadership team. There was a great deal of confusion throughout the team on what results mattered most. Many members of the team shared that a culture of fear existed, and it was stifling innovation. When we presented the findings to John and his team he said, "I'm really having a hard time with this. Should I be taking this personally?" His team immediately came to his defense. One leader spoke up and said, "No John, it's not you. It's just how this culture has been for years." John paused for a moment as he digested the comment and then responded, "No, I think we all ought to be taking this personally. None of this will change if we don't." Flexibility and agility require looking for the perspectives of others. We must open our minds as we review data. We must be willing to acknowledge reality.

BE MOVEABLE

The second question to consider in assessing your flexibility or agility as a leader is to ask yourself:

How moveable am I?

Score yourself 1 to 10 on this question as well. Better yet, have others with whom you work closely rate you on these questions.

On this question a score of 1 means you're a boulder that's not going anywhere. A 10 means you're more like a sailboat headed wherever the wind is taking you.

Being moveable is a choice to avoid the rigid stubbornness that destroys innovation. You constantly ask why and reassess boundaries. "I want people, when they realize they have been wrong about the world to feel not embarrassment, but that childlike sense of wonder, inspiration, and curiosity that I remember from the circus, and that I still get every time I discover I have been wrong," Hans Rosling wrote in his book *Factfulness: Ten Reasons We're Wrong About the World*.

We both once worked with a leader who decided to change the compensation structure for everyone on his team. The leader did not engage or create discussion with anyone on the team as he considered the adjustment. Instead, he made the decision based on what he saw work well at a previous employer. When he announced the change, it went over like a lead balloon. Everyone on the team was frustrated. No one saw anything positive about the change. When the leader started to hear the reality of complete discontent on the team, he flatly denied it. His truth was the only truth. In a virtual meeting the week after he announced the change, he started a team meeting by addressing the pushback to the change. "I am not interested in having a conversation about this topic. You all need to know I am not moveable on this. I need you all to trust me on this change. I am done talking about it," he announced with emotion.

Seven months later, after some of his most senior people left and others threatened to leave, the leader finally budged. He changed the compensation plan back to the way it had been previously. To his credit, he finally became moveable. Unfortunately, his stubbornness had damaged his team's culture and led to some of his best talent departing or being disengaged.

Being moveable requires you to resist the temptation to always be right or always have the answer. Great leaders create space for others. Curious leaders acknowledge reality and are moveable.

ACT QUICKLY

The third and final question to consider in assessing your flexibility or agility as a leader is to ask yourself:

How well am I doing at Act Quickly?

We recommend you score yourself 1 to 10 on this question. Give yourself a 1 if most people think your middle name is Turtle, or you're still using an AOL email address. (We were going to say, "if you're still using an Android phone," but we figured that would tick off a decent chunk of readers, so we'll keep our Apple Fanboy status confidential.) Give yourself a 10 on this question if when baggy clothes started coming back into fashion, you donated everything in your closet to Goodwill and bought XXL everything.

All joking aside, let's agree that agility is the ability to think fast and move fast. We love Amazon's Leadership Principle called "Bias For Action." Jeff Bezos and his leadership team defined the Bias For Action this way: "Speed matters in business. Many decisions and actions are reversible and do not need extensive study. We value calculated risk taking."

A multi-national manufacturing company we work with produces some of the best-selling guacamole products in US grocery stores. In the weeks after the COVID-19 pandemic sent everyone home and cancelled any gatherings of more than five to ten people, the company realized their guacamole products needed to be reconfigured immediately. The company generated significant revenue from party-sized offerings. Those wouldn't be needed by any consumers for months. Their factories needed to immediately shift to individual-sized packs. In a virtual meeting several months into the pandemic, the CEO highlighted his expanded leadership team's ability to think fast and move fast. "That's the type of agility we need in all areas of our company. We have to be willing and able to innovate quickly if we're going to expand our market share," he said.

The third question is designed to measure your bias toward action. You might have an attitude of flexibility but struggle to demonstrate it. Ask members of your team to score you as a leader on this one. You might consider having them provide examples of where you've struggled or excelled at acting quickly.

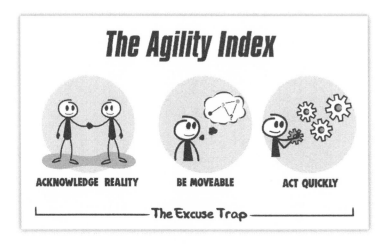

The Agility Index

ACKNOWLEDGE REALITY   BE MOVEABLE   ACT QUICKLY

The Excuse Trap

THE EXCUSE TRAP®

Now for a warning. The great preventor of change is the excuse. Excuses blind us to reality. They justify our lack of being moveable. Excuses help us feel better about delaying action. Our brain wants to find the path of least resistance, and that means continuing to do what it's doing. One of the default mechanisms the brain uses to facilitate this process is serve up all sorts of excuses. We call it The Excuse Trap®. Excuses allow us to opt out of taking accountability. They allow us to focus on things we don't control. Excuses are human nature. We don't have to look far to find evidence to justify our lack of flexibility or agility.

As you consider the massive shift in the workplace toward greater flexibility, we caution you to avoid making excuses for wanting to return to the way things have always been. Leaders who fail to acknowledge reality, aren't moveable, and don't act quickly will find plenty of excuses to justify their behavior. What they will struggle to find at the same time are high-quality employees who want to continue working for them.

THE PUNCHLINE

 **THE DATA:**

- Eighty-three percent of workers want a hybrid model of work. They want to spend part of their week in the office and part at home. They want the flexibility to determine how much time is spent in both places and don't want someone far removed dictating it.
- Twenty percent of employees said they worked from home at least some portion of the time pre-2020. Seventy-seven percent said they worked at home at some point during 2020.
- Asked about their biggest concern in the new hybrid workplace, 32 percent of executives said culture was their top concern. The next highest concerns were productivity (26 percent) and collaboration (19 percent).

 THINK ABOUT:

- The organizations that will struggle the most to retain talent in this new hybrid environment are those who are most directive in where and when someone must work.
- Some of your employees value connection more than others. Some value freedom and being able to work quietly. The greater flexibility you provide them the easier attracting and retaining the best talent will be.
- Working from home changed what time people went to the gym, how often they ate dinner with their families, how much time they spent with their children, and how much of their day was spent commuting. Most employees

don't want to go back to what work looked like pre-pandemic. The future of work has changed.

- Consider how you well you're demonstrating the three elements that measure flexibility on The Agility Index®:
  - Acknowledge Reality
  - Be Moveable
  - Act Quickly

 WHAT TO DO:

- Acknowledge reality. Consider the needs of your team. Ask what's important to them. Give them as much flexibility as possible.
- Score yourself and your team, or better yet have your team score you using the questions from The Agility Index®. You might collect the scores as they relate to a key business problem, priority, or project:
  - Acknowledge Reality: How willing am I/we to acknowledge reality?
  - Be Moveable: How moveable am I/we?
  - Act Quickly: How well am I/we doing at acting quickly?
- Consider how much time you're spending in the Excuse Trap®. How much time are you focusing on what you can't control?
- What narratives have developed on your team that are serving as excuses halting forward progress on critical issues or results?
- Consider how much concern you have about when, where, and how your team works. Evaluate how much of that concern is valid and how much is old thinking.
- Think about two or three things you could change that would provide your team greater flexibility on controlling their schedule and how they deliver what matters most.

CHAPTER SIX

VALIDATE DIVERSITY

Jennifer Brown is a lesbian New Yorker who has sometimes found herself struggling to find a way to say what she's really thinking in conference rooms surrounded by older white heterosexual men.

Wanda Jones Yeatman is a black executive with long dreadlocks who has found herself telling a coworker to please not pet her hair. It's a behavior she says reminds her of what slaveowners did to her ancestors as they decided what price they'd offer to purchase them.

Timothy Clark is a white male Oxford graduate who in his first year as an executive found himself standing on the front porch of an employee's home. He was there to inform the family that their dad and husband had tragically died at work that day. The cause of the accident that killed him? A culture of fear of speaking up.

Much of this chapter will come from these three instead of us. They have unique perspectives and wisdom due to personal experience or years of scholarly research on the topics of diversity, inclusion, and belonging. We're anxious to share with you their incredible insight, stories, and recommendations on how you might lead your team in a way that retains your key talent. We'll turn this chapter over to them in a few pages but first we've got to broaden this topic out from how you might be interpreting the title of the chapter.

THE DATA:

🦻 **86%**

PERCENTAGE OF EMPLOYEES WHO SAY PEOPLE IN THEIR COMPANY AREN'T HEARD EQUALLY.

The Workforce Institute

While people of color, those in the LGBTQ+ community, and women face the most extreme and frequent challenges with inclusion that must addressed with greater urgency, the data shows they aren't the only ones who are not feeling seen or heard in most workplaces.

Much of the discontent we talked about in Chapter 3 that has existed in most companies for years has come from people wondering why they were hired for their experience and wisdom and then asked to quiet down and just "do your job." The level of tolerance for that kind of culture is diminishing. People simply won't put up with it any longer. Unfortunately, most of us are creating that kind of environment on our teams. Diversity and inclusion aren't just about who you hire. They're about whether you're actually listening to them.

"I DON'T HAVE TIME FOR THEIR CONCERNS"

The executive who oversaw all the distribution centers throughout one of Minnesota's biggest employers began one of our monthly coaching calls by abruptly announcing, "I know you're going to tell me this wasn't a good move, but I had to do it." We laughed and asked what she meant. "We had to roll out a new policy to all the centers. I sent an email letting everyone know what the new expectations are. They're not going to like it," she said. "I don't have time to answer their questions or deal with their concerns right now, and I know you're going to tell me that's not a smart move."

The last time we had been on site with her leadership team, we had spent time trying to help them see the difference between creating awareness and creating alignment on a team. Think of the difference between awareness and alignment for a moment. What does a leader do when they want to make someone aware of something like a result they have to hit, a new project, or a policy change? Alignment never comes through one-way communication. If you want your team to be aware of something, you send them an email or announce it in a meeting. You share your screen and show a couple of slides.

What does a leader do if they want to create alignment? Alignment comes through discussion. It requires asking questions and listening.

Involvement leads to ownership and accountability. Don't ask me to take accountability for a decision you made without involving me. And yet we do it every day.

Alignment comes when leaders put up a slide showing a new result and then ask, "What questions do you have?" They don't continue talking until their team speaks up, pushes back, seeks clarity, resolves concerns, and processes it all out loud. Teams that aren't aligned aren't engaged. Alignment demands effort on the part of the leader. Diversity on a team is evidenced in the form of differing experiences and beliefs. Inclusion and belonging occur when leaders seek to listen *constantly*.

We'll share a three-step process that we've seen dramatically impact the level of engagement by all members of a team when leaders follow it. The Feedback Loop® will come later in this chapter, but first we need to practice what we're preaching here. We sought out the perspectives of others on this topic of how to validate the diversity that exists on teams from three people we've met as we've travelled the globe working with thousands of leaders. We want you to hear their experiences and beliefs.

WHAT RACISM LOOKS LIKE

In the days following the death of George Floyd in Minneapolis, we called an executive we respect and admire based on our work with her over the last several years. She's someone who works in a predominantly white male hierarchal culture. The fact that she chose to work there speaks volumes about her courage and boldness. She speaks truth no matter who is in the room and does it in a unique way that turns heads and builds consensus.

"I live in a pretty white world. I'm married to a white man. I have white-passing children. I live in a white neighborhood," Wanda Jones Yeatman said to us. "I don't go out by myself at night anymore. My parents live about five hours away. I take the train to see them."

There are Wandas in every company. And we all need to be listening to them. For far too long, those of us who are white have failed to invite our black coworkers to bring their whole selves to work. How can we pretend what happens in the streets doesn't affect them in the office? And yet when was the last time you participated in a conversation about race at work? When was the last time you, as a leader, facilitated a discussion that validated feelings held by employees about race?

"I had a conversation with one of my kids just today and they were crying and saying, 'why did it take people seeing this man dying for them to care?' She's like, 'it's happened for years. Why did it take that? Why did you have to see it to believe it," Wanda said to us.

We wanted to know what lessons leaders in companies should be learning from the emotion that boiled up and onto the streets around racism in the middle of the global pandemic. Her reaction to our question—a question from white friends of hers—was packed with emotion. "It's not my job to teach you. It's your job to find out. It's not my job to fix racism. It's yours. It's your system. It's your people. You are the ones who benefit from systemic racism. And it is your job to fix it," she said.

"One of my leaders had a meeting where people were able to share where they're at. Just how people are doing on all ends of spectrum. **It's uncomfortable for white people but let's talk about it. If you treat it like it's uncomfortable, then it's uncomfortable.**"

Several times in our conversation with Wanda, she mentioned microaggressions that she had experienced during her career at work. Towards the end of our call, we asked if she could give us an example of what she meant.

"Microaggression would be touching my hair without my permission because you want to know what it feels like. I have dreads, so people are very curious about that, and I've had people touch my hair before, and I've said 'don't touch my hair.' About the third time they did it, I said 'don't touch my hair. I'm not a dog for you to pet. I'm not something you own. Let me explain to you why that's so important to me. Because your ancestors owned my ancestors, and the way they knew if they wanted to purchase me or not was I'd be up on a block and they'd walk around and touch parts of my body as if I was an animal for purchase. So when you touch me without my invitation or my permission, you are exerting a certain level of that same energy of ownership. So, don't touch my hair,'" she said.

In the months before COVID-19 began spreading around the globe, and before the marches in the streets after George Floyd's senseless death, we had an experience that had never happened to us before. We were in a hotel ballroom meeting with the top forty leaders of a company with more than seven thousand employees. The executives spent two days getting aligned around a set of shifts that were needed in their culture. Near the end of the meeting, this group of leaders decided they needed to add another shift. They titled it "Advance Equity." The definition they wrote was, "I create an environment inclusive for diverse individuals and perspectives to enhance and harmonize our work with the communities we serve."

In all our years working with companies we had never had an organization specifically call out equity or inclusion as one of the six or seven most important shifts needed in their culture.

DIVERSITY IS OFTEN NOT VISIBLE

Jennifer Brown wrote the book on *How to Be an Inclusive Leader*. Literally! After we read it, we wanted to hear more about her experiences, so we asked to meet with her. Jennifer is on a mission to teach leaders that diversity isn't always visible. After all, she's a lesbian, which isn't exactly something she announces when she enters a room or logs into a Microsoft Teams meeting.

"I say to myself I need to practice what I preach and acknowledge there's so much diversity in every room. It might not be visible. It's my job to create enough psychological safety so that we can actually get to it," Jennifer told us. "Executive leaders can intellectualize a lot about diversity. They read the business case. There's tons of data on why it's better for the bottom line and performance and stock market returns and all sorts of things. But, I think the personal connection to this is what really needs to be achieved."

"People will come up to me and share diversity dimensions that aren't visible to me like, 'Oh, I'm Jewish, and this is a largely Christian company.' 'I didn't graduate from college and my kids don't even know.' 'My kid is an addict. And we've had so much pain around that,' or, 'I grew up incredibly poor.' You know, I, it's just fascinating to hear the things that people feel safe to share with me after you open the door to that. We want to see a leader being vulnerable and honest and authentic. And that means we can trust that person and follow them and feel comfortable and psychological safety around them," Jennifer said.

We're including this topic in this book because if you want to retain your best talent as employees, you need to create a space where they feel comfortable being authentic. Why? Because that provides an environment where people bring all of their ideas, all of their experience, all of their passion, all of their best effort. They will be loyal to you as a leader and work harder to be aligned to what you ask them to do.

But how do you do that? How do we as leaders create an environment where people feel safe being their true self?

HOW TO CREATE PSYCHOLOGICAL SAFETY

While Tim Clark was working on his PhD at Oxford, he accepted a job at one of the largest steel manufacturing companies in the United States. In his first days on the job, something tragic happened.

"Two workers made one little mistake. They broke a safety rule. One of the workers was killed," Tim recounted. "I was asked to accompany the CEO and inform this gentleman's wife and family that he wouldn't be coming home that day. As you can imagine, that was a defining experience for me personally and professionally. It was an epiphany moment for me when I had my hard hat on and I came to understand what we now know as psychological safety."

An investigation revealed the deadly accident was caused in part by a fear of speaking up. Safety protocols were being violated but no one spoke up and pointed it out. Why? They feared the repercussions that might come from raising their hand. That aspect of the culture had ultimately led to death.

"If leaders are managing and leading by fear, they induce helplessness into the culture. People wait around to be told what to do. Or they make mistakes or break rules and don't tell anybody. Innovation is the lifeblood of growth. In a fear-based organization people can't speak up and challenge. If they can't do that you're not going anywhere as a company," Tim said.

"Most leaders are in denial. All you have to do is ask them to reflect on the last week. Ask them, 'When did you invite challenge? When did your people push you? When did they rock the status quo? How did you emotionally react to that?' It comes back to your behavior as a leader in these moments of truth. How do you emotionally respond to dissent? Do you welcome it? Do you accommodate it? Do you encourage it? There's a lot of denial that goes on, because leaders hide behind title position and authority instead of going out there and saying, 'Let's innovate!' But they have a vested interest in the status quo. The status quo provides incentives that many senior leaders want to keep in place, in terms of rank, compensation, rewards. Often, they even know that competitive advantage is melting. The bottom line is this. When it comes to innovation, the leader is either leading the way or getting in the way. The leader is never neutral in that process."

Dr. Clark has now spent decades studying psychological safety. We asked him to share with us some best practices he's seen in leaders who create a no-fear culture.

"You have to understand that we as humans go into social situations and the first thing we do is threat detection. Your people want to know is this environment safe? If it's safe, then I'm playing offense. If it's safe they I will engage in acts of vulnerability such as asking a question. If it's unsafe now I'm playing defense. I'm not going to challenge. I'm not going to push. I have to manage personal risk. It's about self-preservation and loss avoidance."

"One of the first things I recommend to a leader is don't run your meetings. Give the reins to someone else. Shut up and watch! Listen. Pay attention to team dynamics. Pay attention to interpersonal patterns you see. Are people playing offense or defense? The other thing you're going to do is never speak first. Never! Because your positional power has veto power. It's too powerful. You need to wait."

Tim told us that his research shows only 8 percent of teams have what he calls "challenger safety," where employees feel comfortable challenging the status quo.

"In order to innovate, you need intellectual friction. You need ideas colliding. You need creative abrasion and constructive dissent. The leader's job is to get that intellectual friction up so that we can innovate and solve problems and come up with solutions. At the same time, you need to keep the social friction down because humans are sensitive."

"If the conversation or dialogue gets personal or disrespectful that social friction will shut down your intellection friction. The best leaders I'm around keep intellectual friction really high and social friction really low. If you can do that, watch out! Your team will perform beyond your expectations."

How good is that! We told you we were bringing you three experts in this space, and they absolutely delivered.

THE FEEDBACK LOOP®

Stories and experiences like those we just heard exist in every organization. We haven't heard them because we do more talking than listening. If we had to identify one skill that we believe is underdeveloped in most leaders we've met over the years, it would be listening. When we say "listening," we don't mean being willing to listen. We mean seeking the perspective of others. Leaders who create alignment have developed systems for hearing others. We call that system The Feedback Loop®.

SEEK PERSPECTIVE

The first step in creating an environment where people feel heard and where diversity and inclusion exist is seeking the perspectives of others. That means asking their opinion before you make decisions. Whose opinion should you seek? Anyone who will be affected by a decision or who you're asking to help deliver a particular result or work on a project. Some of you might say, "I have thousands of people under me who work on certain projects or are affected by policies we create. How in the world am I supposed to listen to each one of them? That's insane." Here's how you do it. You give your team of direct reports the opportunity to be heard. You ask them to create the same experience for their team. Those directors or managers are asked to do the same. And so it goes across the org chart. The companies with the healthiest culture have employees at every level who feel heard. How? Because of what we've just described. The leaders at the highest level create an environment where leaders are expected to seek the perspectives of their team. They're expected to listen.

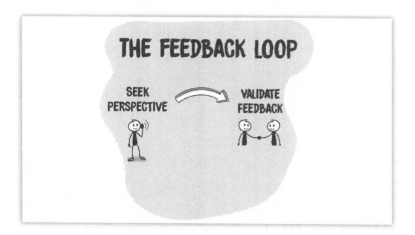

THE FEEDBACK LOOP

SEEK PERSPECTIVE

VALIDATE FEEDBACK

VALIDATE FEEDBACK

Seeking someone's perspective starts the process of being heard but it doesn't complete it. We were in a meeting recently where an executive—let's call him "Phil"—was sharing his perspective when he was cut off by the executive sitting next to him. Let's call him "David." David disagreed with Phil and abruptly interrupted him and started challenging his perspective. We interrupted both of them and provided some structure to the conversation so that both felt validated. We asked Phil to finish what he was saying. For the next several minutes he shared a couple of recent experiences that he felt the group needed to be aware of as they considered the decision in front of them.

When Phil was finished, we asked David if he would summarize what he had heard Phil say. David did exactly that. Phil added a little more detail and David acknowledged he hadn't been aware of the details he had just heard and expressed appreciation for Phil's perspective.

That's what we mean when we say "Validate Feedback." Too often we ask people to weigh in on a topic and give them scant time to share their perspective. We cut them off or immediately begin our rebuttal. Their comment creates a need in our brains to strengthen our argument. When we do, the other person feels anything but validated. We sought their perspective and then destroyed it. We invalidate everything they say. We walk away from the experience patting ourselves on the back for leading such a robust debate, but they leave full of resentment and determine to stay quiet next time.

Validating feedback isn't agreeing with it. It simply means acknowledging it. Showing that you heard it. Demonstrating interest and curiosity in the experiences and beliefs of others. You hired people for their wisdom. Listen to it and validate it.

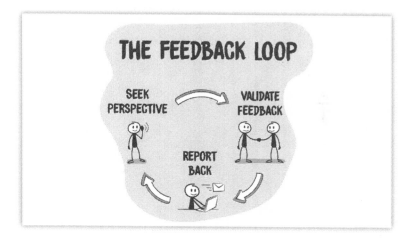

REPORT BACK

The third step is to Report Back. This simply means to follow up. In the story we shared of David and Phil, it's David texting or pulling Phil aside within the next week and letting him know how his input influenced the decision. Reporting back can happen hours or weeks after you receive feedback or insight from someone. It could be as simple as a sentence or two in an email announcing a new policy. "We want to thank the sales managers for their valuable feedback as we considered the new marketing strategy. Their concern about adding pepper to our new toothpaste flavor caused us to do a little more research and discover customers actually don't want it." We kid, but you get the point.

We do make decisions after seeking the perspectives of others, but too often we leave out acknowledging the contribution when announcing the changes. We thank someone for their feedback in a call but then never interpret for them why we did the opposite of what they recommended. Reporting back is a step too many leaders skip, and then they wonder why they don't get any credit or alignment from the time they spent listening to others. Don't skip this third and important step of The Feedback Loop®!

TIPS FROM THE MASTER LISTENER

In this chapter on listening, we have one more voice we want you to hear. Julian Treasure is one of the world's experts on listening. We had a conversation with him that deeply affected us. We all think we're good listeners, but Julian helps us see why so many on our teams and in our lives don't feel heard or seen. Julian lives in Scotland. We sought him out years ago to help us become more effective at coaching executives. Rather than interpret what he told us, we'll simply ask him to finish this chapter.

Julian Treasure:

Sound is incredibly important. It's something I've been aware of, for a very long time, I guess. I'm a musician. When playing in a band, you have to listen to all the instruments at the same time. So, musicians develop a kind of much more particular listening.

Along the way, I started thinking about how unconscious we've all become about listening. Listening is an incredibly important skill, especially for leaders of people or people who are trying to inspire. It's possibly the most important skill of all, and yet, we don't teach it in schools. Think about it. We teach and test reading and writing. It's a scandal if a child leaves school unable to read or write. We do not teach and test speaking and listening, which is strange, because we've been doing those for a lot longer.

I started to use the phrase, 'we're losing our listening.' That became the substance of my third TED Talk, which was all about conscious listening and the fact that our listening is under threat from all these different things. And I perceived, to be honest, that there was a need for somebody to stand up and start shouting about this because a world without listening is a pretty dire world. It's a dangerous world.

Listening creates understanding. Listening creates intimacy. Listening is how you can inspire people and know people.

Without listening, we're on a slippery slope of caricature and hatred and bigotry. A lot of the polarization we've seen in politics in the last couple of years in my country, and your country, is simply about people not listening to one another. So, I think listening is incredibly important in society, in organizations, and not least in families and between friends and relatives. It's a skill. It's a skill you can develop. And it's something that most people hardly think about.

Listening is fundamental to having a motivated workforce in any organization. They say there are three basic human needs in any relationship at work or home. We want to be heard, to be understood and to be valued. If you're not listened to, two of those are right out the window. And the third one follows pretty quickly afterwards. If you can't get listened to, you feel that your point of view, your contributions, your inspirations, your complaints are meeting a dead wall. It's very demotivating for people.

Listening has got a couple of unique factors. The way you listen is a two-step process. Step one is selection. Of all the sounds around you, you select what it is you're going to pay attention to. Step two is even more important. You make it mean something. So my definition of listening is making meaning from sound.

You assign different sounds different meaning. An alarm, your phone, or the voice of your spouse. There are sounds that will immediately grab your attention. Your name, for example, in a crowded room. Other sounds may be new ones. You have to assign them a given value.

That's how listening works. It's selecting what you hear and assigning it meaning. Your listening is different than anybody else's on this planet. So is mine. It's as unique as your fingerprints, your iris, or your voice. Your listening changes over time.

Your assumptions, your expectations, your intentions, all of these things affect how you as an individual listen.

A listening culture in a company is a wonderful thing to create. It takes a lot of efforts from the top down. You can end up with an organization that listens so well. And my goodness, think of the effect on customer service, on sales, on leadership qualities. It's unbelievable. And if you ask any great salesperson, what's the most important part of a sales conversation, they should say it's listening. It's not the speaking, but it's the listening bit. Because that's how you know what the person needs and how you can satisfy them. So listening from top to bottom, it's just incredible when you get an organization that changes like that and has a listening culture.

THE PUNCHLINE

 THE DATA:

- Eighty-seven percent of employees surveyed in 2021 said they didn't feel that people in their company were listened to equally.
- One of the biggest drivers of discontent (Chapter 3) is a lack of being asked for your perspective or feeling like it matters.
- Seventy-seven percent of L&D and HR leaders say diversity, inclusion, and belonging are a higher priority in their companies than they were a year ago. Effort is being made. The question is: What impact is it having?

 THINK ABOUT:

- Consider what efforts you've made to make your team more diverse. Keep in mind diversity is both visible and invisible.
- Consider what efforts you consistently make to help your team feel inclusion and belonging. What do you do to help them have involvement in your decisions? Do you tend to listen to the perspectives of some more than others? Who might not feel heard?
- What experiences have you created to help people feel they can be their authentic self at work?

 **WHAT TO DO:**

- Acknowledge reality. On a scale of 1 to 10, rate the level of diversity of your team. Consider gender, race, age, sexual orientation, ethnicity, education, work experience, origin, and longevity at our organization.
- What could you do to help the team become even more diverse moving forward?
- Consider what steps of The Feedback Loop® you consistently demonstrate:
    - Seek perspectives
    - Validate feedback
    - Report Back
- Consider what steps you need to work on demonstrating more often?
- What meeting or call do you have on your schedule in the next two to three days where you could seek the perspectives of others?

CHAPTER SEVEN

COLLABORATE SELECTIVELY

The company desperately needed to make digital transformation a higher priority. It had been talked about for years, but customers were increasingly complaining that the products and services weren't keeping up with their digital needs. Russ decided to get involved. He wanted to be part of the solution.

The CEO was thrilled. He welcomed Russ's help and requested he fly out to the company's headquarters and spend a few days creating alignment with the team located there and then jumpstart the project. It didn't take long for Russ to realize the problem. Every department had their own vision of what digital transformation looked like and no one was the decision maker.

Within days of getting involved in the project, Russ's calendar was destroyed. He was inundated with invites to back-to-back virtual meetings every day of the workweek. Most of the meetings involved the same people. Some included vendors who were being paid significant sums of money but weren't producing much value. When Russ pressed on the vendors, they complained that they were thoroughly confused and desperately needed a sense of direction on specifically what the company wanted from them and when.

Russ started making decisions. The CEO had asked him to drive the project forward and take the lead. Immediately complaints were made. Executives who disagreed with various decisions demanded more discussion. Employees whose pet projects weren't identified as priorities started sabotaging the effort. "Russ, some on the team are complaining that you're not collaborative enough," the CEO said. "We need you to slow down and make sure everyone agrees with the direction," he said. Russ sought feedback from the CEO on how he could be more collaborative. He showed him how many meetings he had with the people complaining about not being included. "Just keep them feeling good about it, Russ," said the CEO as they wrapped up their call.

Russ individually called each member of the team. He listened. He invested countless hours on evenings and weekends on calls with everyone involved. And then he realized the problem was a cultural one. The culture of the teams involved in the project valued collaboration higher than progress. Discussion was more important than decisions. There was no win here unless the senior executives of the company wanted to change the culture. It turned out they did not. Russ asked to be removed from the project and return full-time to his main job of working with clients. Years later, that company is still discussing how to get started with its digital transformation.

COLLABORATION HAS GOTTEN OUT OF CONTROL

The transition to work from home and hybrid work has people feeling overwhelmed—not at the amount of work they must do, but with anxiety about when they are supposed to get it done. In December 2019, Zoom averaged 10 million participants per day logging into meetings. In mid-2021, that number had increased to more than 300 million people per day.

Microsoft has voiced concern about what it's seeing in companies using its software tools. "This barrage of communications is unstructured and mostly unplanned, with 62 percent of calls and meetings unscheduled or conducted ad hoc. And workers are feeling the pressure to keep up," Microsoft reported after reviewing stats from its customers. The company said 40 billion more emails were sent in Outlook in February 2021 than in February 2020. They reported the average amount of time people were spending in Microsoft Teams meetings was up 148 percent year to year. Microsoft's research shows that, "one in five global survey respondents say their employer doesn't care about their work-life balance. Fifty-four percent feel overworked. Thirty-nine percent feel exhausted."

THE DATA:

▶ **2900%**

INCREASE IN AVERAGE NUMBER OF PEOPLE ATTENDING ZOOM MEETINGS DAILY (NOVEMBER 2019 TO MID 2021)

Zoom Statistics

While we were writing this chapter, we noticed we had two meetings that were added to our calendars by one of our clients (same team, same company). We thought the invites might have been duplicates.

We logged into the first meeting. Half a dozen executives showed up and the discussion was productive. The following morning, we logged into the next meeting with the same group on the invite. When we logged in, no one else was in the virtual meeting room. We waited and wondered if maybe the meeting wasn't happening. Several minutes later, one executive showed up. She asked us about our day and engaged in small talk about the weather for several minutes. She told us she wasn't sure if anyone else would be coming. We brought up an item we wanted to discuss with the group. As the discussion got underway, two other executives showed up. One was on camera but stayed muted the whole time. The other never turned on her camera or unmuted. We're not sure she was really listening.

About ten minutes into the meeting, it was clear there was no agenda for the meeting, and no one was sure who had called it. We were anxious to return to projects we were working on, but didn't want to appear distracted to this Fortune 50 client. The casual conversation continued for another thirty minutes when one of the leaders said, "well, I think we're done. Oh, wait, is this meeting set up for an hour? Oh, sorry, let's keep going." We were polite but wrapped up the conversation and logged off. Two minutes later we got an email from one of the invitees who had just logged in and wondered if the meeting had been cancelled.

This is not healthy or productive! This is not what effective collaboration looks like.

Consider this chapter our manifesto to leaders everywhere to be the change we all want to see in the world!

Stop scheduling virtual meetings just because you can. Stop inviting people just because they might want to be included. Stop staying silent and enabling this to happen in your company.

THE COLLABORATION MAP®

We want to introduce you to a process that breaks down what effective collaboration looks like. It's made of four simple steps that we've taught leaders and it hangs in the conference rooms or is pinned on the bulletin board in home offices of executives we've worked with. It provides what most teams and companies lack. It's a process that defines what effective collaboration looks like. It produces clarity and alignment on teams at scale.

Step One: Define

Define the decision that needs to be made.
Define who will be the decision-maker.

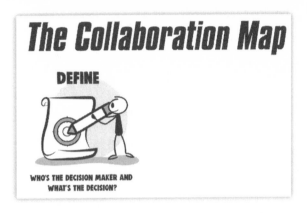

Consider you're invited to a meeting, and on the agenda or in the invite, both of these items are made clear. You know what decision this meeting has been scheduled to discuss. You know who in the meeting has been designated as the person who will make that decision.

Can you even imagine what that would feel like? It's giving you goosebumps right now, isn't it? You're kind of giddy, right? What a shame! How off the rails have we become in most companies that we get excited at the idea of a meeting with that kind of clarity about how the time will be spent?

Most leaders—and most companies—fail to recognize that groups don't make decisions. Groups are terrible at making decisions! Groups inform the leader who will make the decision. That's why a bunch of cavemen and women ultimately decided to create this thing we call a leader. Someone needed to break the tie. Someone needed to be picked, appointed, or allowed to make the decision. The job of everyone else in the tribe was to share their perspective with the head caveperson so they could make decisions that helped keep danger out there and food in here.

Stop assigning groups to make decisions! The group will participate in the discussion and inform the person who you assign to make the decision. That person might be picked because they're the most senior person on the team. They might be picked because they're the most experienced or skilled on the topic being discussed. Or they might be chosen because you want to develop them, or they're closest to the customer.

Leaders are paid to make decisions. The smartest leaders surround themselves with diverse and experienced people, and then seek their input so they make the best decisions possible. If you're invited to participate in a meeting but aren't the decision-maker your role is clear. Accept and embrace it! Your job is to inform the decision maker. It's not to make the decision.

Step Two: Discuss

Invite the appropriate people to be part of the discussion. Invite them all to be heard.

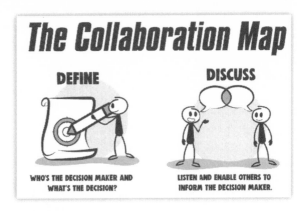

Involvement leads to ownership. Leaders often wonder why people aren't taking accountability for a policy, result, or decision. The reason is often because they feel their perspective wasn't considered in the process that led to the policy change, the result they're now told to deliver, or the decision that affects how they do their work.

Some of us tend to err on the side of inviting too many people to the discussion. This has become far more common as work has become more virtual or remote. Invite a cross section of the people that will be impacted by the decision and those who can provide the best insight on the topic. Others of us lean toward not inviting enough people. This is less common, but some leaders are guilty of doing it consistently. It leads to a lack of alignment and ownership of decisions.

Be aware of your tendencies here and strike the sweet spot between inviting too many and inviting too few. The two measures of decisions are speed and quality. Leaning too hard into speed leads to a lack of alignment and inefficiencies due to missing data. Leaning too hard into quality leads to a lack of innovation and speed to market.

Allow time for enough discussion. Make a point of asking those who don't readily offer their perspectives to speak up. Their silence is rarely due to alignment. It's usually due to a belief that the decision maker won't value their perspective or that they'll pay a price for speaking up.

Step Three: Decide

Make the decision.
Or, call for the decision.

Once everyone invited to participate in the discussion has been heard, it's time to make the decision. If you're the decision maker, this step is as simple and clear as validating the perspectives you've heard during the discussion and then announcing your decision. If you're not the decision maker, you should call for the decision once everyone has been heard.

Our experience is that decisions rarely improve when they're delayed.

We're reminded of Amazon's Leadership Principle, Bias for Action, that we mentioned in Chapter 5. The company trains its leaders that "Speed matters in business. Many decisions and actions are reversible and do not need extensive study. We value calculated risk taking." We see far more companies and leaders that are Biased for Discussion than Biased for Action. You've heard the perspective of your team. They've shared data with you. Now, make the decision! That's your job as a leader.

Step Four: Own

Own the decision as if you made it yourself.

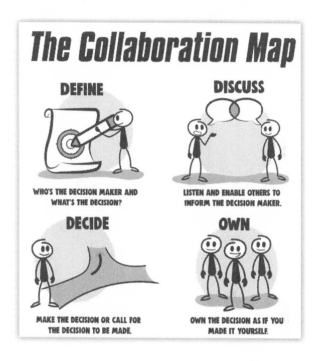

Nothing destroys alignment more than someone logging out of a meeting and then actively seeking to sabotage a decision made in the meeting. They say things like, "I spoke up against that decision in our meeting," or "I can't believe they made that decision; I told them it wasn't going to work." The goal of the discussion leading up to the decision isn't to get the team in agreement. In fact, we hate that word. Hardly anyone agrees on anything! Leaders don't seek agreement. They seek alignment. If you've been heard, it's time to get aligned to the decision. Own the decision as if you made it yourself!

There are exceptions, but they're extremely rare. In cases where the decision is unethical or illegal, it should go without saying that you shouldn't get aligned to it but rather report it to the appropriate people. If the decision is one that you feel is taking the company in the wrong direction and something you just can't support, then it's likely time to consider leaving the organization. What you don't want to do is undermine the decision. To complain about it. To turn negative and resentful. If you simply can't take ownership of decisions that are being made, it's time to depart.

TOO MUCH VS. TOO LITTLE COLLABORATION

For years most companies have sought to find a way to encourage more collaboration. Talk of silos and competing priorities in various departments or teams slow down innovation, negatively affect the customer experience, and lead to a culture where it's hard to retain the best talent. And yet, a newer phenomenon is the complaint of too much collaboration. Talk of too many meetings and a tsunami of emails, chat, and invites leads to feelings of being overwhelmed and overworked.

Most employees actually feel both. Most companies are struggling with both. **There are too many silos and far too much collaboration. That's why we chose to title this chapter "Collaborate Selectively."** We are encouraging less activity and more intentional collaboration. Less activity will help ease the discontent we've documented in this book and that you already knew existed all around you. More intentional collaboration will help break down barriers, create greater clarity and alignment, and increase speed to market and customer satisfaction. All of that will better position you as a leader to attract and retain the best talent in this era of The Great Resignation.

We've got one more thought we've been told by others has helped them visualize what it means to Collaborate Selectively, or effectively.

Most of us tend to gravitate to one end of what we call Collaboration Styles®. On one end of the spectrum are those we call **Discuss & Analyze**. On the other end of the spectrum are people we'll call **Decide & Act**. You already know which one you are, don't you?"

Discuss & Analyze

Those who have this Collaboration Style have never received an invite for a meeting they didn't want to confirm. They place a high value on hearing the perspectives of others. They tend to ask lots of questions. There's nothing they love more than a PowerPoint slide with tons of bullet points. These leaders view their style as a major strength. They see others around them acting too hastily or struggling to build consensus. These leaders don't struggle with any of that. They have never driven the company off course. Or maybe they did once, and they've sworn never to do it again. If you work for a leader like this, you already know what will be on next week's meeting agenda. It will be the same two to three issues that have been on the agenda for the last two years.

The strengths of this Collaboration Style are the inclusion scores. No one feels like they're being overlooked or not heard. Everyone feels like they get a chance to weigh in before decisions are made. Surprises rarely happen here. Alignment is high. The challenges with this style are speed and innovation. People start to become disengaged because of the leader's inability or unwillingness to make decisions. The team starts talking offline about how slow things are moving and how much time they feel they're wasting.

Decide & Act

On the other end of the spectrum is the Collaboration Style® of those who pride themselves on moving fast. These are leaders who often make decisions without ever having any discussion with anyone. Members of their team and other departments scan their email inbox everyday wondering what surprises will pop up today. New policies come out all the time. Compensation plans and bonus structures change almost quarterly. Employees who everyone thought were in good standing are fired or reassigned so frequently that people wonder if they're safe. Leaders with this style hate meetings. They think nothing of skipping some of those on their calendar. And if they do ask your opinion, it feels like they're doing it to check some box.

The strength of leaders with this Collaboration Style is that they tend to be on top of market trends. They are committed to never being out innovated or accused of being complacent. They—and their teams—learn a ton from trial and error. Companies, departments, and teams led by these types of people are incredible at speed to market. These leaders are efficient to an extreme and waste no one's time. No one complains about too many meetings or meetings that go over. The challenges to this style are a complete lack of alignment and a total absence of inclusion. No one has any idea what will happen next and the anxiety level on the team is palpable.

The Sweet Spot

So, which Collaboration Style is better? The answer is both! The sweet spot is a moving target somewhere in the middle. We say moving target because the market is never stagnant. In the moments immediately following the global shutdown due to COVID-19, companies needed leaders who were able to lean hard toward Decide & Act. In many instances the survival of companies or business units depended on a leader's ability to make decisions fast. Alignment wasn't nearly as important as action. This was especially true in the healthcare space where decisions were literally the difference between life and death. Other industries needed decisive action and very little discussion as well. Think of restaurants that had to shift to all curbside pickup, delivery, and drive-thru interactions with customers. Airlines, retailers, and manufacturers faced decisions with enormous repercussions. Leaders unable to move quickly saw their personal leadership stock tank instantly.

That kind of situation doesn't show up every day, though. And leaders who get stuck too far on the spectrum toward Decide & Act find their ability to deliver short term results is remarkable while they struggle mightily to retain the best people and build alignment far and wide. Leaders who can't create clarity and alignment don't scale. Thus, being willing to demonstrate some of the attributes of the Discuss & Analyze style is critical.

THE PUNCHLINE

 **THE DATA:**

- The number of people attending meetings on Zoom jumped 2900 percent from November 2019 to mid-2021. More than 300 million people were logging into meetings daily.
- Forty billion more Microsoft Outlook emails were sent in February 2021 than in February 2020.
- Microsoft reported the average person was spending 148 percent more time logged into virtual meetings on the Microsoft Teams platform in 2021 than in 2020.
- Surveys universally reported employees feeling greater anxiety, more stress, and being overwhelmed.

 THINK ABOUT:

- Employees are spending far more time in virtual meetings, answering emails, and on company chat tools then they did pre-pandemic.
- The additional interaction has not led to greater levels of trust or feelings of improved cross-functional collaboration.
- The data shows we're getting collaboration all wrong. The answer isn't more meetings with more people in them. The solution is having a collaboration framework.

- The collaboration framework we've built after being asked to help leaders on this topic for years is called The Collaboration Map®. It includes these steps:
  - Define:
    - Get clarity on what decision needs to be made.
    - Get clarity on who will be the decision-maker.
  - Discuss:
    - Invite the appropriate people to be part of the discussion.
    - Make sure everyone has been heard.
  - Decide:
    - Make the decision once the appropriate people have been heard.
    - If you're not the decision-maker, call for the decision to be made.
  - Own:
    - Own the decision as if you made it yourself.
- Consider we all lean toward one of two Collaboration Styles®:
  - Discuss & Analyze
  - Decide & Act

 WHAT TO DO:

- Acknowledge reality. Are you inviting people to too many meetings? Are you leaving others enough time in their day to execute decisions and actually get their work done? Consider asking your team or those you work with most to share their perspective on the level of collaboration and discussion happening now.
- Memorize The Collaboration Map® or create your own collaboration framework that provides a defined process

for making decisions. Remember, alignment comes from involvement. Don't ask your team to own decisions you don't involve them in.

- Consider what Collaboration Style® you lean toward. See if others are aligned with your self-assessment. Consider which direction on the spectrum you need to move and what experiences you can create to get closer to the sweet spot between the two.

CHAPTER EIGHT

PRIORITIZE & FOCUS

Sally couldn't wait to show us what was in the conference room. The moment we showed up at the company headquarters where she worked, she excitedly asked us to follow her down the hallway. One of the long walls alongside the conference room table was a floor-to-ceiling white board. The board had been attacked by a whole variety of colored dry-erase markers and was covered with words, phrases, and drawings. There was literally no white space left on the massive white board.

Sally bragged to us about how many fabulous ideas her team had captured on the board during their recent full-day brainstorm session. It was good to see how pleased she was at the creativity and wealth of ideas her team had generated. As she smiled and pointed at the wall, we asked what we thought was a natural question. "Which of these great ideas did you you decide to pursue? Sally, looked confused by the question and even insulted by it.

Sally responded, "All of them!"

All of them? Yes! She said her team left the meeting planning to focus on all of the ideas on the wall. As tragic as this story sounds, it happens everywhere. KPI might be the worst three letters ever stacked together. How can 150 things be "KEY" Performance Indicators?

The leader who is trying to deliver it all rarely delivers what matters most. Effective leaders narrow their team's focus.

It's hard to reach a destination if the leader wants to drive down every side street. Your team needs clarity and focus. And they need it now more than ever in this remote and hybrid environment! The most experienced, talented, and high potential employees want to work for leaders who create clarity around what matters.

THE NURSING HUDDLE

In the days before COVID transformed hospitals in ways they never expected, we sometimes found ourselves in nursing huddles making observations for executives who hired us to assess the culture. During one visit to a hospital in Virginia, Jared was invited by a nursing supervisor to attend the 7 a.m. huddle that happens every morning at shift change. The overnight team briefed the daytime crew on things that happened during their shift that those coming on duty needed to know about. This particular area of the hospital was the Oncology Unit, where patients are typically fighting serious diseases.

Jared listened as the nurses exchanged information on patients and then watched as the leader finished the huddle pointing to a bulletin board. She said, "I want to do a quick update on our scorecard." She pointed to one sheet of paper stapled to the board. Then another. Then another. Jared started feeling dizzy. As he looked at the clinicians and staff in the huddle, Jared noticed they had that glazed-over look in their eyes—and not just the ones about to go home. No one seemed to care at all about that scorecard.

When people are given too much information, they actually shut down. Research shows people can focus on three to five things at any given time. The metrics on all those sheets of paper at that hospital were important. We're not recommending ignoring all metrics at the expense of a few. We are suggesting that the best leaders take the complex and make it simple. Focus is what differentiates the teams that achieve extraordinary results from those that are busy but not moving the needle.

> **THE DATA:**
>
> ◎ **84%**
>
> **PERCENTAGE WHO SAY THEIR ORGANIZATION'S RESULTS AREN'T CLEARLY DEFINED**
>
> Workplace Study

It's hard to hold people accountable for delivering results when more than eight out of ten of them aren't clear on what they are.

Leaders tell us over and over that their teams need to be more strategic. Most aren't strategic because they are focused on reacting to the tactical obstacles that pop up every day. They're measuring their success by how much activity they're engaged in. They feel busy. Their days are packed full of emails to respond to, meetings to attend, calls to make, and things to do. We talk about wanting hardworking employees. Well, they are!

DESCRIBE THE DESTINATION

The problem is that most leaders aren't leading their teams anywhere. They haven't defined the destination. And if they have, they rarely mention it. All your team hears you talk about are the activities that need to get done. How many meetings in the last week or month have included a minute or two from you talking about the destination?

When we say the "Destination" we're talking about one or two outcomes that define success three to five years from now. It might be a revenue number. It could be a membership or customer metric. We've seen organizations define their destination as Zero Emissions, $1 billion in revenue, 30 percent market share, 10 percent growth in margin, or become a Top 20 Training Company.

The best employees want to work for a leader who is taking their team somewhere. They're on a mission. They can see the promised land and are working to lead their team there. That begins by defining the destination. In our experience it's rarely productive to go out more than three years to pick a target. Some organizations we work with in the space or automobile manufacturing industries have a vision they're working toward that requires looking out eight to ten years. Those companies are the exceptions. Most of us should be defining a destination that's not as far into the future.

WHAT ARE YOUR ANNUAL KEY RESULTS?

The late Andy Grove was the pioneer of the term *Key Results*. He brought the concept to Intel back in the 1980s. From there it spread throughout Silicon Valley. For decades, Key Results have been a set of metrics that companies use to create clarity and alignment on teams around what needs to happen in the next twelve months to keep the organization on the path to its long-term destination.

"When people have conflicting priorities or unclear, meaningless, or arbitrarily shifting goals, they become frustrated, cynical, and demotivated," wrote venture capitalist John Doerr in his book about how tech companies use Key Results to create focus. "An effective goal-setting system starts at the top, with leaders who invest the time and energy to choose what counts. There are so many people working so hard and achieving so little."

Key Results aren't descriptive. They don't describe how we need to work. They don't sound like "collaborate more," "communicate effectively," or "wow the customer." Key Results are the most important outcomes that ultimately define our success this year.

Each results that is one of your Key Results should be measurable. You want your team to be able to recall these without any assistance. The Key Results in any given year are so engrained in some of the organizations we work with that nearly all forty thousand people in a business unit could tell you what they are if you quizzed them without warning. They serve as the definition of success. Here are a few examples:

- **GROWTH**: Increase revenue 10 percent
- **SAFETY**: Zero accidents today
- **PEOPLE**: Strengthen employee retention to 90 percent
- **CUSTOMER**: Improve NPS 15 percent
- **PATIENT SATISFACTION**: Achieve top quartile in HCAPS
- **QUALITY**: Reduce defects by 18 percent

Key Results create alignment of what matters most. They help teams and individuals know what to focus their energy and activity on. They create prioritization. As a leader, you might be tracking fifty or more different metrics. Each of them tells you something, and is therefore important, but they aren't equal. As a leader, you help your team most by providing them with the three or four outcomes that are the top priorities.

As you work to define the Key Results, keep in mind that there's no such thing as a perfect metric. Don't waste time or get wrapped around the axle discussing the perfect measure is for the "People" category, or the "Safety" category. Pick the best one you have and go with it!

One of the drivers of discontent that's fueling The Great Resignation is the lack of focus and clear priorities coming from leaders. When employees work remotely, they need even more help knowing where to focus their time and energy.

Key Results provide that clarity. If you're working on something that doesn't move the needle on one of the Key Results maybe you should set it aside or stop.

ESTABLISHING CRITICAL EXPECTATIONS

In the months after the pandemic began, many executives we worked with gave us feedback that their teams needed even more help understanding where to focus their time in the short-term. Employees who had less access to each other and their leaders wanted greater clarity on exactly what was expected in the next thirty to ninety days. This was something we hadn't heard a lot about pre-COVID. And yet we received a ton of feedback in the first half of 2021 from leaders who said establishing Critical Expectations made a huge difference on their teams.

Critical Expectations are those things that people need to focus on in the short term. We'll give you a few examples. In April 2020, we were on the phone with "Mike," the head of sales for a food manufacturing company we first mentioned in the Introduction of this book. Mike's division had hundreds of sales reps spread out across the country. Their primary customers were universities, hotels, and restaurants.

Think back to those early days of the COVID pandemic and the impact on university campuses, on the travel industry, and in restaurants. All three became ghost towns. Suddenly, Mike's division, which was crushing their year-to-date results at the time, was dealing with massive disruption and uncertainty. They had warehouses producing tons of meat and food products ready to be shipped to customers who were suddenly cancelling their orders. In that first call with Mike after the pandemic hit, he sounded exactly how you'd expect: deeply concerned. "We have a saying in this business that if you don't sell the product, you smell the product," Mike said.

We asked, "is your team clear on what you expect them to be doing right now?" After some discussion he realized they probably weren't. In a meeting on Zoom with the entire sales force, Mike kicked off the meeting announcing the Critical Expectation of "5 by 25." He explained that he needed every sales rep to contact five potential customers who had never done business with the company by the twenty-fifth day of the next month. Within minutes hundreds of Mike's sales reps had clarity on what they needed to do starting immediately. These expectations roll up to the Key Results, by the way. Mike's Critical Expectation of 5 by 25 was directly related to his team's Revenue Key Result for the year. In the summer of 2021, Mike told us that he has decided to establish Critical Expectations every quarter for his team. "They help everyone know what we need them focused on right now. We have three of them at a time," Mike said.

HIERARCHY OF CRITICAL EXPECTATIONS

"People think focus means saying yes to the thing you've got to focus on. But that's not what it means at all. It means saying no to the hundred other good ideas that there are. You have to pick carefully. I'm actually as proud of the things we haven't done as the things we have done. Innovation is saying no to 1,000 things," Steve Jobs, the co-founder of Apple, said.

Critical Expectations not only establish what's urgent and will have the most impact, they also help people to know what to say 'no' to or to stop spending time on. As you consider what two or three things might need to be Critical Expectations for your team, consider what you need them doing that's both urgent and impactful.

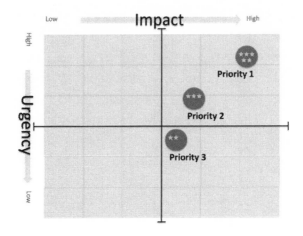

These Critical Expectations should be established using a process that leads to alignment not just awareness, as we discussed in Chapter 4. You want your team bought in and not feeling like they're mandates that some executive dreamed up as a total waste of their time and energy. Allow the team to help create them and then make sure they're on meeting agendas and discussed frequently. Have people share stories in meetings and on calls of where they're having success.

WHAT FOCUS AND PRIORITIZATION LOOKS LIKE

Think of the difference that exists on teams when employees have clarity around what matters most, where the organization is headed, what metrics are most important, and where they should focus their energy in the next ninety days. That's a team we all want to work on. It's a leader who creates an environment that attracts and retains the best talent.

To recap, here's what focus and prioritization looks like:

1. Describe the Destination
- What are one or two metrics that capture where we're headed in the next three to five years?

2. Define the Key Results
- What are the three most important outcomes we have to hit this year?
- Make sure you establish them with a category and metric for each one.

3. Create Critical Expectations
- What are two or three expectations we need members of the team to accomplish in the next thirty to ninety days?

THE PUNCHLINE

 ### THE DATA:

- Eighty-four percent of employees say their organization's results aren't clearly defined
- Good leaders are taking their teams somewhere. They've defined the destination.
- Balanced scorecards don't help employees know what results matter most. Key Results create clarity and alignment around what teams and individuals should prioritize.
- Critical Expectations help employees working in hybrid or remote environments know what their leaders need done in the next thirty to ninety days.

THINK ABOUT:

- Consider whether you have defined the destination for your team. What one metric, if reached in the next three to five years, would define success and generate something your team can rally around?
- What are the three or four most important outcomes your team has to deliver in the next twelve months? These don't describe how your team needs to work but rather what you need to deliver. Remember: There are no perfect metrics. Pick the best one!
- Employees value knowing what they should prioritize. Without help defining Critical Expectations they tend to overvalue activity rather than accomplishing the Key Results.

 **WHAT TO DO:**

- Acknowledge reality. Have you clearly defined the destination for your team? Do they know exactly what to deliver in the next three to five years. If not, pick a metric that defines success and helps your team fulfill its purpose.
- Ask a few members of the team privately what two or three results are most important for the team to deliver this year? Ask them what number the team is shooting for in each of those areas. See how much alignment currently exists.
- Consider whether your team could benefit from having a set of Critical Expectations. If so, pick two or three things everyone needs to do in the next thirty to ninety days that would accelerate achieving the annual Key Results.

CHAPTER NINE

CUSTOMER OBSESSED

He scooted his chair up to the table, looked forward at the couple dozen people in suits and skirts facing him, and then his eyes moved down to the printed pages in front of him. He spoke calmly yet confidently into the microphone on the table.

"My mom had me when she was a seventeen-year-old high school student. It was difficult for her. When they tried to kick her out of school, my grandfather went to bat for her. After some negotiation, the principal said, 'OK, she can stay and finish high school, but she can't do any extracurricular activities, and she can't have a locker.' My grandfather took the deal and my mother finished high school."

The man took a breath and then continued. "My dad's name is Miguel. He adopted me when I was four years old. He was sixteen when he came to the United States from Cuba. My dad arrived in America alone. His parents felt he'd be safer here. His mom imagined America would be cold, so she made him a jacket sewn entirely out of cleaning cloths, the only material they had on hand. We still have that jacket."

Jeff wanted his audience to understand his roots. He wanted to humanize himself after he had gained a title no one else had: "the world's richest person."

A few minutes later, Jeff Bezos shared with the US Congressional Committee what he credited for the unparalleled success of the company he founded. Amazon now has more than one million employees. Five hundred thousand positions were created in one year: 2020! (That's 1,369 new hires per day, for those doing the math.)

 Fun fact: the company received more than 384,000 job applications in one day alone: September 16, 2020. (Mind blown, right?) Ok, back to Bezos in front of Congress."

"Customers are always beautifully, wonderfully dissatisfied, even when they report being happy and business is great. Even when they don't yet know it, customers want something better."

"A constant desire to delight customers drives us to constantly invent on their behalf. No customer ever asked Amazon to create the Prime membership program, but it turns out they wanted it. Not every business takes this customer-first approach, but we do, and it's our greatest strength," Bezos said.

It's Amazon's greatest strength because it not only affects revenue and innovation but also affects their ability to retain quality employees. Wait, how? Glad you asked. Our research into attracting and retaining the best people continually took us to the same starting point: the customer.

In our first trip to South Lake, Washington, we were skeptical of what we heard Bezos say publicly. His word choice was cute. Describing customers as "beautifully, wonderfully dissatisfied" is the type of thing an executive says in front of Congress, but step into one of their internal meetings and it won't take long to hear very different adjectives used to describe customers—if you hear them brought up at all.

We had been invited to Amazon City—otherwise known as downtown Seattle—to run a couple days of strategic sessions that would be attended by hundreds of Amazon leaders. We were surprised at the invite since the word "consultant" is a profane term in Bezosland. But somehow we were given security badges.

In the weeks leading up to this meeting, we studied everything we could find about Amazon's culture. You can't Google that phrase without finding tons of references to Amazon's Leadership Principles. We've mentioned one of them already in this book. We wanted to review the first one here.

Customer Obsession: Leaders start with the customer and work backwards. They work vigorously to earn and keep customer trust. Although leaders pay attention to competitors, they obsess over customers.

Impressive, right? But then again, how many companies write fancy statements like this at management offsites and then fail to operationalize them? We intended to spend part of first two days at Amazon probing to see if this mindset really existed. It turns out we didn't have to do any digging. Within minutes of the meeting starting the word "customer" came up over and over again. No matter what topic was brought up, everyone in the room insisted it be considered from the customer's perspective. It was as if the boss of this team was the customer. We had never witnessed leaders of an organization talk about their customer more.

Where groups in other companies worry how their decisions will be received by leaders above them or around them on the org chart, this group in downtown Seattle was fixated on how the customer would interpret everything they do. Within mere minutes of gaining access to Amazon's headquarters, we were sold. This company was different. It truly was Customer Obsessed!

Cultures like that don't happen by accident. They are created. But how? And how does this all this talk about customers help you retain your best people? Glad you asked. We're headed toward answering that question. We saved this chapter for last because it's what we want you thinking about as you finish this book—the customer.

TWO VERY DIFFERENT HOSPITALS

The largest hospital chain in the United States asked us to travel to Virginia to figure out why two of their hospitals just a few miles apart from each other were having such different results. We took a team from our firm and spent half the day at one hospital and half at the other. Our time was spent interviewing dozens of employees and doing what's called "leader rounding" in various units. That's where you go to the maternity or surgery units with employees walking from room to room checking on patients, while spending the time between rooms checking on the employee. Asking them questions about how their jobs are going and hearing what's on their minds.

In both hospitals one of the questions we asked every employee we interacted with was:

"What is the biggest obstacle to higher patient satisfaction scores at this hospital?"

In the hospital with poor results, no one, not a single person in over twenty-five straight interviews, hesitated to answer that question. They all responded, "we need more people." In the hospital with exceptional results, the question was greeted by silence and contemplation. There was no consistent answer.

We were stunned at the difference between the two groups. But then as we analyzed our conversations at both hospitals in greater detail, we noticed another—and even more significant—difference. In the poorly performing hospital, we noticed one word was rarely mentioned by the employees we talked with. The word was "patient." In the other hospital the word was uttered frequently by their team members.

The hospital with poor results had the more toxic environment. The staff universally blamed their outcomes on not having enough people, and were so focused on internal problems that they rarely brought up the word "patient" in their conversations with outsiders. We discovered that the hospital with better results had the same employee to patient ratio but had a culture focused on patients. Collaboration, accountability, and communication were at a whole different level in the higher-performing hospital.

Keep in mind, both of these hospitals were owned by the same company with the same policies, budgets, and resources. Both were in the same city and the same part of town separated by only a few miles. The only difference we could find between the two were their leadership teams.

Think of the advantages companies and teams experience when they make the customer, patient, or member their core focus. They innovate faster. There's less blame. There's greater collaboration. Better decisions are made.

The further the customer is from the minds of employees, the more toxic the culture is on that team.

The more internally focused a team becomes, the worse their results trend over time. Pick any company that's fallen off a cliff or slowly declined, and you'll see how easy it is to gather exhibits for our argument. Revenue and profit are lagging indicators. There are leading indicators of success and trouble. Two of them are employee engagement and employee retention. Both decline when people feel like they're caught in bureaucratic molasses chained down by policy after policy and stuck in meeting after meeting. Creativity and communication are stifled and it's not long before the most talented people start heading for the exits.

Disruptive companies become such because of their proximity to the customer. Their access to the customer allows them to adjust faster to the increasingly frequent shifts in customer demands. That's an environment that attracts the best talent. Growth attracts talent and growth comes from giving the market what it wants.

WORKING IN OZ

Years ago the two of us worked for two amazing people. They were best friends who had written a book together called *The Oz Principle*. The book became a hit. It made *The New York Times* bestseller list. Executives read it and wanted their entire company trained on the principles contained in it. When we joined this fast-growing consulting firm, we would dial into company conference calls or attend company meetings where most of the time was spent discussing what was happening with our customers. Our bosses peppered us with questions about what challenges the executives we were consulting with were having. **They wanted to know what value we were bringing our clients and what struggles we were having serving them.**

Very little time in our meetings was spent reviewing sales dashboards or revenue numbers. Sure, they were discussed, and financial performance mattered. But it wasn't a major focus of our discussions. We spent most of our time in meetings talking about customers. We brainstormed new models or thinking that could help our clients solve their biggest problems. We told stories of their successes. We collaborated on their challenges. The two of us left those calls and meetings energized. We loved what we did for a living. We loved who we worked for. We were completely engaged. Everyone was completely engaged. We were on a mission to help our clients achieve greater success. It's what mattered more than anything else.

THE DATA:

♡ **85%**

EMPLOYEES WHO ARE
UNSURE THEY CAN LIVE
THEIR PURPOSE IN THEIR
EXISTING JOB

McKinsey & Company Research

Looking back, we now realize how unique that period of time was that we worked for Roger Connors and Tom Smith—the coauthors of *The Oz Principle*. **Their decision to run the company in a way that was obsessed with the customer created a culture focused on others rather than ourselves.** Revenues grew every year. We had no marketing department. Our clients were our best marketers. As they were promoted and changed companies, they took us with them. Eventually we found ourselves working with the leaders of Amazon, Walmart, Lockheed Martin, Cigna, Johnson & Johnson, Kohler, HCA, Darden Restaurants, Southwest Airlines, and the list goes on and on. The secret of the growth of that company internally and externally was its focus on the customer.

SATISFIED EMPLOYEES & SATISFIED CUSTOMERS

Fred Reichheld had a question. The year was 1993. Fred wanted to know if there was a way to predict whether a customer would purchase from a company. Fred was working at the consulting powerhouse Bain & Company, leading a research team. He decided he needed to investigate a few companies to answer his question.

One of his first stops was Atlanta and a fast-growing restaurant chain that had one main product: a chicken patty and two slices of pickle on a bun. How was a company with such a basic product experiencing explosive growth? The restaurant business was growing at an annual rate of 3.4 percent, but Chick-fil-A's sales were climbing 15 percent. Out of fifty-three years of existence, the company had only had one year when same-store sales declined.

Fred started to uncover more statistics about Chick-fil-A that caught his attention. "What made them interesting is their store operators stayed for twenty years in the same job. That's five-percent turnover rates. Why would you want to stay in the same fast-food job for twenty years? I called some of them and asked them. They said 'because we're proud to work in an organization that treats people the way we do at Chick-fil-A and we make three or four times as much money as if we worked at the competition,'" Fred said.

"Do you know what the average operator makes in their industry? They make $50,000. But Chick-fil-A's average store operator earns $170,000. That's the average. Averages are very misleading. What about the top dozen or so? They earn over $400,000 a year. Running a chicken sandwich shop! I dismissed it as an odd ball myself at the time. I missed the underlying truth. They run a loy-alty-based operation and it generates a set of economics that most people cannot see."

Chick-fil-A has the highest customer satisfaction scores in the restaurant industry. No one comes close. The other metric that no one in their space can compete with is sales per location. Chick-fil-A leads that category. The nearest fast-food competitor is McDonalds which generates 50 percent of Chick-fil-A's average.

No company is perfect, and Chick-fil-A has generated its fair share of controversy over the years, but no one who has spent time in their drive-throughs or restaurants would dispute that the experience was remarkably different than getting food from any other fast-food chain. **Dee Ann Turner, the head of Human Resources at Chick-fil-A for three decades, told us, "We became the number one customer service brand in America. And the way you become a brand like that is you have extraordinary talent.** That talent is well-trained. You have teenagers saying 'my pleasure' and going the extra mile for their customers and exceeding their expectations. If you want to have great customer service, then you go find the best employees."

Jimmy Collins, the long-time president of Chick-fil-A, described himself to us as a disciple of Truett Cathy—the founder. Collins was in his thirties when he decided to join Cathy's company. That process began on a Friday night in Truett's original restaurant located a few miles away from the massive Atlanta airport. "Truett chatted with me as he took my carryout order. He asked, 'How many people will be eating?' I answered, 'There will be six of us.' When he handed me the bag of food, he also handed me a whole lemon meringue pie, and said, 'Have dessert on me.' I was flabbergasted! We did not eat there often, and Truett hardly knew us. It is my first definite memory of the person, Truett Cathy." Consider for a moment that it was Truett's commitment to customer satisfaction that attracted the executive he would lean on for thirty years to help run his company and create one of the greatest stories ever in the restaurant industry.

LESSONS FROM RENTAL CARS

Fred Reichheld was impressed by what he found at Chick-fil-A, but the Bain researcher needed more data in his quest to find the predictor of customer loyalty. So, he headed to St. Louis— the home of Enterprise Rent-A-Car. Enterprise was developing a reputation for low prices, high customer satisfaction scores, and was quickly gaining market share. The company was founded by Jack Taylor and named after the aircraft carrier he served on during WWII. As Jack got older, he handed the reigns to his son, Andy.

"I went out to St. Louis and asked Andy Taylor, 'what's the secret of your success?' He said, 'we think loyalty is at the core of it because we figured out there's only one way to grow a business. Take care of your customers and your employees first, and the profits will follow.' It sounded so midwestern. I wondered, what's going on here? What I didn't know is how you can afford to over-pay your people 30 percent or more, which is what Enterprise does, and charge less to your customers and generate $10 billion of net worth," Fred said.

Enterprise is a business success story that most of us are completely unaware of. They have 44 percent market share. Their nearest competitor, Hertz, has 15 percent. In 2019, Enterprise did $17.8 billion in revenue compared to Hertz's $6.9 billion. They operate the world's largest fleet of vehicles with more than 1.7 million cars, vans, and trucks.

Enterprise doesn't have a single executive who didn't start at the counter in one of its locations. The company doesn't hire leaders from outside. Promotions and compensation are all tied to customer satisfaction scores. "At the corporate office we have this belief that the best ideas come from the field. They're interfacing with customers every day. It's the reason we start everybody at the bottom. The lead dog here is the customer. I'm the CEO not so our people can try to figure out what I'm thinking. I'm here to empower our people and remove obstacles to their ability to succeed. I am serving them," Andy Taylor said in an interview.

After spending time studying Chick-fil-A, Enterprise, Harley Davidson, and other brands with exceptional customer satisfaction, Fred Reichheld and his team at Bain developed a new metric. They called it the Net Promoter Score or NPS. Today virtually every large company and thousands of smaller ones use it to gauge customer loyalty.

"People ask 'why did you get focused on this subject of customer and employee loyalty?' Those two things go together.

I noticed the companies that were admired earned enormous loyalty from customers and employees. Both were proud to be associated with those firms. The other thing I noticed was their financial results were extraordinary.

Companies that earn loyalty don't just talk about it. They measure it. Loyalty drives long-term sustainable growth," Fred said.

WHERE IS YOUR TEAM'S FOCUS?

The most successful and talented people—the kind of people you want on your team—are those who are committed to helping you deliver for the customer. At the end of the day, the customer matters most. Without them your organization has no reason to exist. And yet if you log into meetings and silently listen, how often do you hear the customer mentioned? What is your team's focus?

We have noticed over the years that teams with the fastest speed to market, the ones taking risks and innovating, those where trust

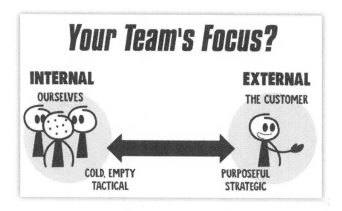

is high and fear is low, and where the culture is a competitive advantage are far more concerned with customers than themselves. Their focus is on what's happening out there. They're externally focused. Their culture feels purposeful. There's unity around their strategy and a drive to execute.

Teams struggling to grow market share, that are slow to change, are mired down by silos, and frustrated by high turnover are often internally focused. Their cultures feel cold and empty. There's no soul. Everything feels very tactical and disconnected. There's no strong sense of purpose and very little unity.

It all comes down to a decision. A decision by you. A decision to focus your team on serving the customer. Delivering for them. Your focus is your team's focus. After all is said and done, a team is a reflection of their leader. How they think and act is a result of your behavior, your expectations, your focus, and what you tolerate. No one matters more than the customer. Your company exists to serve them. As you take care of your people so they can take care of the customer, you will succeed, your team will thrive, and the customer will be loyal.

THE PUNCHLINE

 **THE DATA:**

- Amazon added more than 500,000 new positions in 2020. Yeah, it's a random data nugget but how insane is that?
- Seventy percent of workers said their purpose is driven by what they do for work.
- Eighty-five percent of frontline managers and employees said they were unsure if they can live their purpose in their existing job.

 THINK ABOUT:

- Consider whether your team is focused more internally or externally. Does the discussion in meetings center more on what customers need or on issues and challenges inside the company?
- Consider whether the current culture of your team feels more tactical, cold, and empty or more purposeful and strategic?
- Consider how much you talk about purpose, the long-range target you're leading your team toward, and the needs of the customer in your interactions with employees and in meetings.

 **WHAT TO DO:**

- Acknowledge reality. Where is the focus of your team right now? Is it more internally or externally focused? What could you do to cause the focus to be more on the customer, member, or patient?
- Consider how you speak of the customer. Do you describe them as a nuisance or complain frequently about their shifting needs and high expectations? How could you bring the face of the customer into more meetings?

PART THREE

LEAD
DIFFERENTLY

CHAPTER TEN

WHAT YOU CAN DO STARTING TODAY

One of our friends—he was a coauthor of our last book titled *Remoteability: 12 Tactics to Manage the Culture of Your Suddenly Remote Team*—loves to ask the question, "Therefore, what?" As we wrap up this book, we hear the voice of Tanner Corbridge in our heads. We want to ask his question to you. Now that you know all of this, Therefore, what? What will you do? What should you do?

The next few pages should help you answer that question. We've taken the most important data, the core concepts of each chapter, and all of the models and frameworks we've introduced to you in this book and put them all together in this chapter. We wanted you to have one place where you could go quickly to reference them as you implement whatever you've decided your team needs most. We'll walk you through that on the coming pages.

There's another option as well. As we wrote this book, we presented some of the data from it to leadership teams across the world. These included senior leadership teams of defense contractors, manufacturing companies, and two of the largest global pharmaceutical companies, along with hundreds of people in virtual meetings. They asked questions. They pushed back on some of our findings and suggestions. They shared stories and additional data with us. They gave us ideas. Most importantly, they helped us take what you just read and develop it into a collaborative experience that generates movement. It provides leaders an opportunity to upskill their people management skills to meet the needs of tomorrow's workforce. And we do it all in thirty days.

EXPERIENCE 'LEAD IN 30'

Each month we accept up to 250 people in the Lead In 30 digital cohort experience. This isn't a virtual course. It's not a webinar. It's a fast-paced, action-oriented online collaborative experience. Think of it like a fitness or no-sugar challenge. It's transformative. You'll have access to micro video content to be consumed for a few minutes every day or two and live access to us and some of the experts and executives we've quoted in this book for one hour every week. We'll dig deeper into each chapter and give you items to work on, to try out in meetings or a one-on-one, and then report back in our virtual sessions. You'll be going through it alongside executives and leaders from other companies around the world.

To find out more about the next Lead In 30 cohort go to LeadIn30.com. You can read more about what's included in the experience, see when the next monthly experience kicks off, and reserve a seat for you or your entire leadership team before next month's seats sell out.

We can't wait to meet many of you and work alongside you every week for a month!

 For your company: If you have interest in us doing a customized virtual or in-person session for a team of leaders in your company about the concepts and data in this book, you can find more information about what that could look like and how to contact us at LeadIn30.com.

THE DATA AND FRAMEWORKS

We wrote this book to share the trends we discovered that are changing the future of how we work, and to help leaders around the globe like you adapt in ways that give you a competitive advantage in attracting and recruiting the best talent. On the following pages, we've assembled the most important numbers as well as all the frameworks and models that we've presented throughout the book. We put them all together so that you could quickly reference one section of the book and quickly find any of these visuals as you work to apply what you've read. The way we work has changed. The way we lead must as well.

Introduction

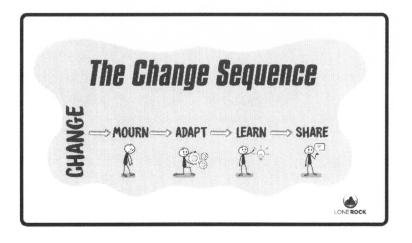

Chapter One: The Seismic Shift

THE DATA:

 41%

PERCENTAGE OF GLOBAL
EMPLOYEES CONSIDERING
LEAVING THEIR JOBS

Microsoft Work Index

THE DATA:

12M

NUMBER OF US EMPLOYEES
WHO QUIT THEIR JOBS IN
JUST THREE MONTHS

U.S. Bureau of Labor Statistics
(April-June 2021)

Chapter Two: The Rise of the Individual

THE DATA:

 **13.7%**

ANNUAL PERSONAL SAVINGS
RATE 2020 (HIGHEST ON
RECORD IN U.S.)

U.S. Bureau of Economic Analysis

THE DATA:

 **$1.9T**

TOTAL MONEY IN
'AMERICAN RESCUE ACT'
IN RESPONSE TO COVID-19

White House

THE DATA:

 0.5%

GROWTH RATE OF
THE U.S. WORKFORCE
(WAS 1.6⬜ 1950-2000)

U.S. Bureau of Labor Statistics

Chapter Three: The Discontent

THE DATA:

1. DISCONTENT
2. SHIFT IN
PRIORITIES

REASONS PEOPLE ARE QUITTING JOBS

Microsoft Work Index & Gallup

THE DATA:

 66%

PEOPLE WHO SAY THEY'RE MORE EFFECTIVE WORKING FROM HOME

Linkedin's Workforce Confidence Data

The Disengagement Cycle

MAKE NOISE

WE DO WHAT WE CAN TO GET THE LEADER'S ATTENTION AND BRING OUR PERSPECTIVE INTO THE LIGHT OF DAY

BLAME OTHERS

FEEL UNDERVALUED AND FRUSTRATED, WE VOCALLY COMPLAIN AND BLAME

GO SILENT

WE'RE DONE. ALL THE HOPE IS LOST AND WE GIVE UP

Chapter Four: Process + People

THE DATA:

 12%

PERCENTAGE OF LEADERS WHO SAY THEY KNOW HOW TO MANAGE ENGAGEMENT & CULTURE

Deloitte Human Capital
Trends Report

Chapter Five: Demonstrate Flexibility

THE DATA:

 20%

PERCENTAGE WHO WORKED AT HOME SOME PORTION OF THEIR WEEK PRE-2020

 71%

PERCENTAGE WHO WORKED AT HOME AT SOME POINT DURING 2020

PEW Research Center

THE DATA:

 83%

PERCENTAGE OF EMPLOYEES WHO WANT A HYBRID WORK MODEL

Accenture Research

THE DATA:

 32%

PERCENTAGE OF EXECUTIVES WHO SAID CULTURE WAS THEIR TOP CONCERN IN THE NEW WORKPLACE. THEIR NEXT HIGHER CONCERN WAS PRODUCTIVITY FOLLOWED BY COLLABORATION.

Deloitte Return to Workplace Survey

The Agility Index

ACKNOWLEDGE REALITY   **BE MOVEABLE**   **ACT QUICKLY**

The Excuse Trap

THE DATA:

73%

EMPLOYEES WHO SAY THEIR COMPANY STRUGGLES TO HEAR THE HARD THINGS.

Workplace Accountability Study

Chapter Six: Validate Diversity

THE DATA:

🦻 **86%**

**PERCENTAGE OF
EMPLOYEES WHO SAY
PEOPLE IN THEIR COMPANY
AREN'T HEARD EQUALLY.**

The Workforce Institute

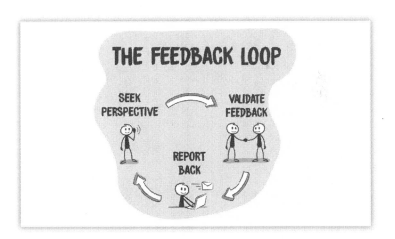

Chapter Seven: Collaborate Selectively

THE DATA:

▶ **2900%**

INCREASE IN AVERAGE NUMBER
OF PEOPLE ATTENDING ZOOM
MEETINGS DAILY (NOVEMBER
2019 TO MID 2021)

Zoom Statistics

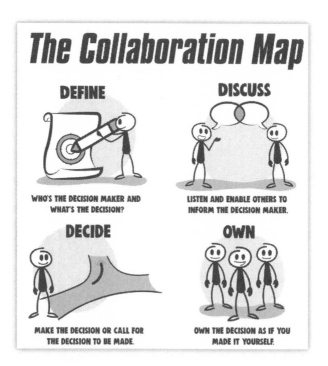

The Collaboration Map

DEFINE

WHO'S THE DECISION MAKER AND
WHAT'S THE DECISION?

DISCUSS

LISTEN AND ENABLE OTHERS TO
INFORM THE DECISION MAKER.

DECIDE

MAKE THE DECISION OR CALL FOR
THE DECISION TO BE MADE.

OWN

OWN THE DECISION AS IF YOU
MADE IT YOURSELF.

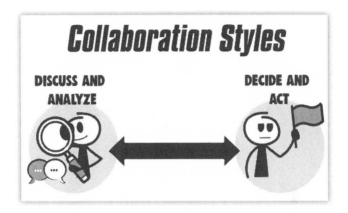

Chapter Eight: Prioritize & Focus

THE DATA:

⊙ **84%**

PERCENTAGE WHO SAY
THEIR ORGANIZATION'S
RESULTS AREN'T
CLEARLY DEFINED

Workplace Study

Chapter Nine: Customer Obsession

THE DATA:

❤ **85%**

**EMPLOYEES WHO ARE
UNSURE THEY CAN LIVE
THEIR PURPOSE IN THEIR
EXISTING JOB**

McKinsey & Company Research

Read on for a free excerpt from the authors' previous book:

Remoteability: 12 Tactics to Manage the Culture of
Your Suddenly Remote Team

INTRODUCTION

R uss was walking out of a meeting in the Washington DC area when a senior executive stopped him and asked, "Why don't we do the next meeting virtually?"

(This book has three co-authors: Russ Hill, Jared Jones, and Tanner Corbridge. That's why you'll read the word "we" a lot in this book. We'll share more about our background in the coming pages, but we should probably get back to Russ's story. He gets mad when we interrupt his stories. That's sarcasm by the way—expect more.)

Russ had just finished facilitating two days of intense discussions among some of the leaders of a Fortune 100 company. The executives were deep in the work of trying to shift their culture to accelerate the results they needed to deliver. Our conversations those two days had been emotional but productive. Most participants had flown in for the meeting at the company's headquarters.

"These meetings don't work virtually. Sorry. We know that would be a lot easier, but we'll need to get everyone back here in person as soon as possible," Russ said, as he wheeled his luggage out of the room and raced off to the airport.

Then, Covid happened.

Guess what Russ discovered? He was wrong. Embarrassingly wrong. (Happens a lot, actually.) Okay, maybe we all held the same belief.

You probably did too. Most of us thought things we did in person wouldn't translate to the virtual world.

Russ and some of our colleagues met again with those executives who were in the meeting near DC more than half a dozen times in the following months. All of those meetings have been virtual. All have been remarkably productive. That company's culture is moving in the right direction. It turns out that culture can be managed effectively remotely! We witnessed it over and over again last year with the diverse set of companies we're privileged to work with.

WHY THIS BOOK?

If you're looking for a book on how to use Zoom, Teams, or WebEx, this ain't that. Sure, we can show you how to unmute yourself before speaking brilliance that no one heard, but our real expertise is in culture management. We—the three co-authors of this book—have nearly four decades of consulting experience with leaders like you on how to manage culture and create accountability for results.

Remoteability isn't just about how to conduct virtual meetings and how to interact with remote teams. It's also about how we engage our people and our customers in a completely different way. Any leader who isn't consciously adjusting their leadership style to this brand-new world is failing to demonstrate remoteability.

Some of you may be reading this thinking the new work environment is temporary. Perhaps you're expecting that in just a few months, everything will be back to normal and everyone will return to their desk in an office building again. You probably thought Covid-19 would be a three-month interruption too, though! Betting against change or disruption is a quick way to lose money.

While none of us can predict the future with certainty, we're pretty confident that work life will never look exactly like it did pre-Covid. This work-from-home genie isn't going back in the bottle. A 2020 Global Workplace Analytics Survey found that 76 percent of people said that they want to continue working remotely after the pandemic ends. If we had to guess, based on our interaction with lots of leaders in lots of companies, we'd predict that a hybrid approach is the future. That hybrid will feature a lot less business travel, a mixture of in-person and virtual meetings, and a schedule comprised of at-home and in-office work weeks. That new environment demands that we all lead differently. Buckle up: We've all got a lot of adjustments to make to how we lead our teams!

THE 10-80-10 PRINCIPLE

We live in a time of constant disruption. (For instance, Jared is a diehard Patriots fan. We like to remind him a lot about the disruption he's been going through.) On a much more serious note, Covid-19 is arguably the biggest disruption in decades. But it's not the only one and it won't be the last. Massive and constant changes in customer and employee expectations are also driving significant disruption.

When disruptions occur, people tend to segment into three groups. (We didn't make up this principle, but we're convinced it's accurate.) It's called the 10-80-10 Principle.

The principle states that when disruption happens, **10 percent of people go into Panic Mode**. This group responds to disruption in one of two ways. They crawl into the fetal position in the corner sucking on a bottle of status quo, hoping their tenure will convince the destroying angel to pass over them. Or they douse their noggin with hair spray, light a match, and scream all kinds of impractical ideas as they run through the house at full speed, hoping their urgency will cause others to think they've "got this." (Someone, please grab the fire extinguisher!)

Another group is made up of **the 80 percent of people who slide into Stunned Mode.** These folks did not expect the disruption and aren't sure what to do in response to it. People in this group aren't paralyzed or crazy but rather are sitting on their hands waiting for someone to tell them what to do. This is the group waiting for the cavalry to come over the distant hilltop and save them, when we actually need them to "saddle up!" They justify their lack of movement with their willingness to innovate or do things differently. They say they're willing to be agile but actually aren't. Part of them doesn't want to commit to trying a "new way" in case it turns out that hard work wasn't really needed. Think of the fad diet crowd, not treadmill warriors. They're head nodders, rather than early adopters. These folks often have great intentions but a ton of muscle memory.

The third group is the roughly **10 percent of people who jump immediately into Create Mode** when disruption strikes. These are the innovators. They are the ones who have been vocal proponents of change for years. They knew the future demanded a new way of doing things and hoped someone would eventually listen to them. The people in this group are totally comfortable driving in fog. Their minds are thinking, "Why pull over and wait when you can slow down a little, turn on the headlights, and keep moving?" The destination is so ingrained in their minds that they literally have never even thought about visiting a rest stop. While the panicked group is freaking out, this group can't believe a moment of opportunity this big has finally arrived.

Keep in mind that where people sit on an org chart has nothing to do with which group they fall into when disruptions hit. We've seen senior executives in Panic Mode and plenty of individual contributors in Create Mode.

The 10-80-10 Principle generates a couple of questions for you:

> **QUESTION ONE:** Which group are you in? (*Are you sure?*)
> **QUESTION TWO:** How do you get more people on your team into Create Mode?

Self-awareness is critical when how we work is changing so dramatically. If you're in Panic Mode, get help fast! Let go of whatever got you to this point in your career because there's no way that it will unlock opportunity in the future or help your team deliver results now. In other words, Panic Mode = Career Killer.

If you're in Stunned Mode, stop waiting for direction! There are two groups that can help you deliver results and bring value immediately: customers and colleagues in Create Mode. Get as close to both as you can and ask tons of questions. Listen to what the customer needs and wants and consider the ideas being proposed by the innovators around you. Where possible, give more visibility and responsibility to those in Create Mode and reassign or part ways with those who are stuck in Panic Mode.

To those of you in Create Mode, keep offering ideas! You must realize that only 10 percent–roughly—of the team or organization is as comfortable as you are in the current environment. Keep talking with customers and speaking up and sharing what you're hearing. Don't wait for permission to try new things—in appropriate ways, of course—and don't slow down! The more you evangelize innovation and how it can immediately impact results, the greater support you'll likely find.

One word of caution for you innovators: Some of your organizations won't survive. As you offer ideas with urgency and patience, some of you will discover that your team, division, or company are led by people who are completely stuck in Panic or Stunned Mode. When and where appropriate, you may have to consider changing where you work. We coach more than a few leaders who have discovered in recent months that their company or boss are in total Panic Mode. Those have been some very tough calls, as we've heard leaders we've built strong relationships with over the years stare at choices that aren't easy.

STORIES OF CHANGE

We feel like we're three of the luckiest people alive. We consult for some incredible companies. You'd recognize the names and brands of many of them. They're well-known restaurant chains, manufacturers, healthcare companies, defense contractors, insurance brands, retailers, and energy companies. Due to non-disclosure agreements, and because lawyers can sound scary, you won't read their names on these pages. But you will hear their stories! Stories about how they're navigating the massive shift to leading remotely. We've spent most of the last year logged into virtual meeting rooms with them as they've dealt with massive shifts in customer demand, supply chain disruptions, resource reduction, reduced travel, employee fatigue, mute buttons, and offices they're now sharing with dogs and kids.

The demands on leaders have never been heavier. A huge amount of uncertainty and unending changes in every aspect of our lives don't relieve us of the expectation to deliver results. But, where's the new leadership playbook? Are there best practices that can help us hit our targets in this newly dispersed work environment?

That's why we wrote this book. We are confident that it will prove to be a <u>practical, timely guide you can quickly consume and immediately implement</u>. The ideas we share here are all designed to do one thing: help you deliver results. We don't advocate focusing on culture because it makes work more fun or enjoyable. Those things are nice byproducts of culture, but they aren't THE reason to work on culture. We work on culture because your team or organization's culture is producing your results.

Managing culture is a skillset that has proven to be a game changer over and over again. The companies we advise hire us to help them shift their culture. We have a combined nearly 40 years of experience consulting for leaders on culture management. Organizations have cultures but so do teams. Your team has a culture. That culture is producing results. If you need different results, then you need shifts in your culture. We wrote this book to help you manage your team's culture—and do it entirely or partially remotely.

Culture is the way people think and act to get things done. When we use the word *culture* in this book, we're not talking about ping pong tables and new perks designed to make people happy. Culture can persuade a 16-year-old high school student in a drive-through to make you believe that she is thrilled you came to order a chicken sandwich and actually cares what your name is! Culture can produce a system that allows you to click a button on your phone and somehow trigger the movement of an item from a gigantic warehouse to your front porch overnight or in a few hours. Culture triggers a decision by a pilot to push a wheelchair down a jet-bridge rather than leave it to someone else to do.

Managing culture isn't a soft skill. It has the potential to be your—we're talking directly to you right now—competitive advantage. Don't be fooled by the thickness of this book. We say this with tons of humility, but what you're holding right now has the potential to be a game changer for you as a leader. How do we know? Because of what we've seen happen when leaders start to intentionally manage their culture. This book will get you started on that path. And it will show you how to do it remotely!

NOW TO THE 12 TACTICS...

So, with that huge expectation raiser (maybe we should have underpromised and overdelivered—hmmmm), we want to walk you through how we structured the pages ahead. We broke this up into 12 tactics. The 12 tactics are things you can do immediately to begin managing the culture of your team. How did we pick these 12? We actually started with five based on observations we made in the first few months of most teams beginning to work at home. We worked with some teams that seemed to be stuck in the Stunned or Panic Mode (some are still there), while others quickly transitioned into the Create Mode. Everyone's game plan was thrown out the window. Some adapted and shifted quickly while others are struggling to get movement and traction.

After presenting what we called "the 5 Leadership Competencies During Uncertainty" in a live webinar that more than 3,000 people participated in, we started helping some of our clients implement them. That exposed additional skills and competencies that were clearly critical to helping remote teams deliver results. Ultimately, our list grew to 12 tactics that we're now ready to share with leaders around the globe.

These are the 12 tactics we see leaders demonstrate that create a culture of delivering results on remote teams:

1. Create clarity.
2. Generate alignment.
3. Build accountability.
4. Be visible.
5. Be accessible.
6. Be transparent.
7. Increase agility.
8. Demonstrate empathy.
9. Manage beliefs.
10. Run effective meetings.
11. Validate authenticity.
12. Ensure your well-being.

Let's go....

To read the full book search Amazon.com for Remoteability: 12 Tactics to Manage the Culture of Your Suddenly Remote Team

Read on for a free excerpt from the Russ's Hill's first book:

Decide to Lead: The Four Questions Anyone Who Wants to Lead Others Must Be Able to Answer

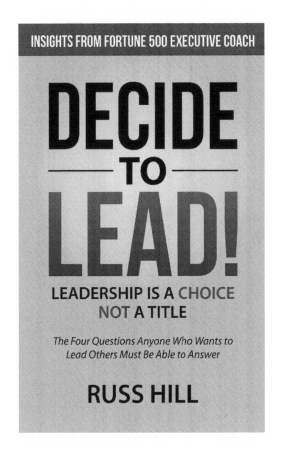

CHAPTER ONE

IT'S YOUR DECISION

One Saturday morning when I was a teenager, I decided to grab our family basketball and head out to the rusty basketball hoop my dad had haphazardly attached above the garage door on our modest two-story home.

As I dribbled the ball on our sloped driveway, a car drove up and stopped. The driver exited the car and started walking toward me. He was dressed in slacks, a button-down shirt, and a tie. I recognized him as someone who attended our church and worked for the local NBC TV station. Everyone in our congregation knew he was the guy on the TV news.

To my surprise, he knew my name! He said, "Russell, I've heard you're interested in the news business. Is that true?"

From my earliest days as a child, I had always wanted to be a news reporter.

"Yeah, that's true," I responded.

"What would you think about maybe coming down to the TV station and spending the day with me sometime?" he asked.

I distinctly remember wondering if I was dreaming. *Was this really happening?* Did this man I hadn't even officially met just ask me to go spend a day in a place I've always wanted to work in?

Two weeks later, Art Rascon drove up to my driveway again. This time instead of wearing shorts and a t-shirt, I was in slacks and a button-down shirt. I climbed into his car and spent the day in the NBC newsroom in downtown San Antonio and riding around in a television news truck.

That experience changed me.

A few years later I began work as a weekend news reporter for a radio station almost no one listened to. I was still in high school and felt like I had launched my path to greatness.

One night after I graduated high school Art called. He now lived in Los Angeles and rioting had broken out after the verdict in the Rodney King trial. Art told me I needed to get on a plane and come to LA immediately to cover what was certain to become a huge story that could propel my career in the news business forward.

Within 24 hours I was in LA doing my first television live news report.

Art went on to become a correspondent for the CBS Evening News. I spent 16 years in the broadcast news business.

It all started on that driveway when I was holding a basketball. Art Rascon made a decision to drive by my home on the way to work and to stop and offer to mentor a nerdy teenager. And in that moment, he became someone who would have a profound impact on my life. He helped lead me where I needed to go and to do what I needed to do in order to start a successful career in broadcast news.

DECIDE TO LEAD

Great leaders often have a major impact on people's lives. They change a person or organization's future. Their influence is like ripples in water. It stretches far and wide often affecting countless people both directly and indirectly. No one can make you a leader. Sure, they can give you responsibility to manage a group of people or they can ask you to help someone else. Yes, they can ask others to listen or report to you. But, they cannot convince others to follow you.

Leadership is a choice.

Whether or not someone becomes a great leader is first determined by their answer to this simple, yet critical question:

Question #1: Do you want to be a leader?

The question is a basic one. It might even seem obvious in a book about leadership. It should not, however, be treated dismissively. The impact of that decision on a person's life is profound. Whether or not someone decides to have children is based, in part, on the answer to that question. Our response to that question drives how we respond when we face obstacles that are taller and wider than we anticipated. Our response determines how much influence we will have on the lives of other people. This first question really comes down to probing how much you want to impact others.

Amazon CEO and founder, Jeff Bezos, was asked in an interview at a business conference in 2018 what it felt like to be the richest man in the world. He said, "I own 16% of Amazon [stock]. Amazon's worth roughly a trillion dollars. That means that what we have built over 20 years. We have built $840 billion wealth for other people. And that's what we've done. That's great and how it should be.'"

Bezos has created a very nice lifestyle for himself to say the least but his decision to be a leader has influenced millions of lives—the lives of customers, employees, and shareholders. If I asked you to consider everyone who has had a significant impact in your life every name you came up with would be someone who made a decision to lead. It might have been a decision they made to lead in a specific moment by doing something that required courage. Or, it could have been their willingness to invest in you by teaching you something, sharing some advice, or sacrificing their time, energy, or substance to positively affect your life.

My friend, Tom Smith, who is one of the co-authors of The Oz Principle, likes to say, "leadership is facilitating movement in the desired direction in a way people feel good about."

The leadership coach and author, John C. Maxwell said, "leadership is not about titles, positions, or flowcharts. It is about one life influencing another."

We use the word leader too casually. We often call people in positions of authority leaders when so many of them are leading us nowhere. Leadership is about getting movement and influencing others. I have been surprised by the number of people in leadership positions I have associated with who have generated hardly any movement or haven't even defined what influence they wish to have on their team or others.

It has been eye-opening to me as I've traveled the world these last several years interacting with tens of thousands of senior executives, directors, and managers just how few of them have had any formal training in leading others. Organizations identify individual contributors who seem committed and elevate them to positions of so-called "leadership" without giving them any help in understanding how to lead people or where they're supposed to be leading their teams to.

These front-line employees are enticed by the higher pay or prestige that comes with a new title and then quickly find themselves frustrated by the fact that people question them, don't follow their policies and directions, and fail to be as committed as they are to the work.

Organizations elevate people to the so-called leadership team or even the senior leadership team who have no clue what it even means to be a leader.

Every week I'm in front of groups of managers speaking to them in groups from 20 to 2,000 depending on the setting. I regularly get sustained applause from these crowds after offering them even the most basic and simplest help in understanding the concept of leadership. We must do a better job of developing leaders. I have devoted the last several years of my life to it and this book is my latest effort along with the weekly podcast I do and the content I push out on social media to help develop more effective leaders.

LEADERSHIP IS ABOUT RESULTS

Jeff was CEO of a food manufacturing company. His company's products are found on the shelves of gas stations, grocery stores, Walmart's, and Costco's. They have plants in the United States and Mexico that employ thousands of people.

By most measures, the company was doing relatively well when Jeff took over as its leader. He's not the complacent type though, and so Jeff started to think about the potential of the company. He had big dreams. Before any of them could be accomplished he decided he needed to address one critical measure: employee engagement. The survey results weren't terrible, but they weren't exceptional either.

Jeff decided his leadership team could change that. He elevated employee engagement to be one of the three metrics the company would use to determine whether or not it had a successful year. The other two were top-line revenue and profit.

With great urgency, Jeff and his senior leadership team, went to work to lift employee morale. Within eight months, the annual survey results were released and the company's performance had significantly improved. They went from being mediocre to best-in-class. In less than 12 months thousands of employees were feeling much better about where they worked and how their teams were being led.

Jeff didn't stop there. As he thought about it he decided a workforce that was more engaged should theoretically be able to produce stronger results. So, he set a goal of 99% fill-rate for orders of frozen burritos, guacamole, salsa, and tortilla chips, among other things that were produced in the company's factories. When Jeff proposed making the fill rate one of the three annual Key Results he was met with skepticism. A 99% fill rate allows hardly any room for mistakes throughout the year.

Twelve months later, the company celebrated another successful employee engagements survey and achieved its goal of a 99% fill-rate!

When Jeff was made CEO of that company no one told him he should make the organization a leader in employee engagement or a model of efficiency in food manufacturing. He decided he wanted to lead his team of thousands of employees to achieve things they had never accomplished before. His decision to lead his organization to a place it had not yet been was intentional. He did it after carefully considering what it would require and the possibility that he would not be successful.

Jeff understood that leadership is all about delivering results. At the end of the day, great leaders move the needle. Their impact is measurable. The job is not to run a meeting or produce a schedule. Leaders mobilize people to deliver different results than they are currently achieving. We'll speak more in the coming pages about how great leaders define their desired results and align people around them.

Before we get too much deeper into the tactical part of this book I want to make sure we're all aligned around the impact of answering Question #1 - *Do You Want To Be A Leader*—with a 'yes.'

THE PRESSURES OF LEADING

"I find one thing very motivating—I love people counting on me. And, so, today it's so easy to be motivated because we have millions of people counting on me," said Amazon's Bezos. Amazon has millions of customers, investors, and now more than half a million employees.

Many of us would find the pressure of all those people depending on us crushing. Some people find it difficult to have anyone counting on them. That's why this book begins with Question #1. Before we can get any deeper into a discussion of what makes someone a great leader we have to draw a line in the sand. On one side of the line are those who are perfectly comfortable being a follower in all areas of their lives. On the other side of the line are those who have a desire—and a willingness—to lead.

The reality is just because you want to be a leader doesn't make you a great leader. It doesn't even make you a decent leader. The world has no shortage of lame—or said in a nicer way, ineffective—leaders.

When you Decide to Lead, you're walking out from behind the curtain and onto the stage under the bright, hot lights. You're leaving the shadows. You're raising your hand. You're leaving the bench and running onto the court ready to grab the ball.

Deciding to lead means you are willing to be criticized, questioned, and challenged in front of everyone. It means you are willing to own the failures. Leadership brings with it a magnifying glass that causes people to not only see but often bring attention to your blemishes, contradictions, and weaknesses.

Being a leader looks easy. Almost everyone thinks they can do it. Walk into any organization and just listen to people talk about all the things the leader of their company should be doing. To them, the best course of action seems so obvious. Employees wonder, how could the leader possibly be so clueless?

Being the leader sometimes totally sucks. There are many days when you'll wonder—is this really worth it?

I've spent my entire life going to church every Sunday. A few years ago, I was asked to serve as the leader of our congregation of more than 500 people. The assignment was temporary—just a few years—and I felt fairly comfortable agreeing to it. After all, I had spent my whole life watching people take turns leading our congregation and I figured I had a good idea of what the position required.

Part of my assignment was managing the charitable funds donated by our members. I was to distribute some of them each month to individuals and families in need. I took this part of my job very seriously. No one wants the money they donate to a church to be wasted.

Late one Sunday I was in my office at the church—remember this was a volunteer assignment as I wasn't paid to do this job that was in addition to my full-time professional job—about to meet with a single mom who relied on financial help from the church for years. It had become obvious that she had become overly dependent on these funds and the assistance was actually damaging her ability to be self-reliant. She couldn't see it but her reliance on others for more than a temporary period of time had lowered her feelings of self-worth, work ethic, and even her health.

Months before this meeting with this wonderful woman I had begun working with her to build a budget and a plan that would enable her to require less assistance from others. Some of her grown kids would move into her place. They would help with some of the bills. She would get a part-time job. There were other elements of the plan as well.

She was very resistant to implementing these changes in her life. She struggled to see how they were helping rather than inconveniencing or even hurting her. Our meeting that evening was for me to gently remind her that the next check she would typically get would not be coming—as we had discussed for months. I spent considerable time rehearsing how I would deliver this message to her. It had to be done in a gentle, loving, and yet resolute way. It would have been so much easier for me to simply write her the check from donated funds. The church had the money. But, how long would this cycle go on? Every time I wrote a check would lead to another month this young woman would sit all day inside her home rather than seek to develop the willpower and work ethic that would lead to the satisfaction and accomplishment of supporting herself.

The meeting began and I kindly delivered the news she had already heard from me before—there would be only one assistance check rather than two checks from the church this month. She began to sob. She became angry at me. She reminded me I had access to funds that could help her. She was confused at what seemed like my lack of compassion. She sat slumped in the chair in front of me and felt tremendous pain from my decision.

After realizing my mind was made-up she stood up and walked out of my office without shaking my hand or any pleasantries. I closed the door and cried. I knew what I had done was ultimately the best thing for this woman and her family but I also knew it would be quite some time before she saw me as anything other than heartless. I was convinced my decision would positively impact the direction of this woman's life but I knew it would take time— likely a long time—before she would see it that way.

The decision to lead others brings with it very difficult moments. In this opening chapter, I just want to keep it real. Yes, leadership brings with it incredibly rewarding moments. We'll talk more about those in the pages ahead. But, it also stretches and tests the leader in ways he or she has usually not experienced previously.

LEADERSHIP MEANS MAKING DECISIONS

Leaders make decisions. Those decisions are often unpopular. If everyone kept doing what they're doing right now no one would ever deliver different results. Leaders facilitate movement. They help influence people to do things they're not currently doing so that the outcome will be different.

Leaders are not passive participants in an organization or on a team. I regularly sit through meetings and interact with a lot of managers who don't take a strong position on the issue being discussed. We pay leaders to make decisions. Groups don't make decisions.

Leaders make decisions. The job of the group is to inform the leader so he or she makes the best decision possible.

Far too often managers view their role as facilitating discussion or helping people do their jobs. That's part of it but it misses a critical element of leadership. When you decide to be a leader you are choosing to put yourself into situations where you will need to make difficult decisions. It is your job to take a position. To choose a path or determine the course of action. Who you choose to surround yourself with will have a huge impact on the quality of the decisions you make. There is a balance great leaders must strike between listening to the opinions of others and shutting off dialogue and confidently making a decision.

Some managers struggle to listen to others. They make decisions without listening to hardly anyone and not interpreting the decisions they make. Others listen to everyone for far too long and seemingly can't get up the nerve or confidence to make the decision.

Think of leadership in its most basic form. Every tribe or group needs someone who is tasked with carrying the flag and leading the way. Groups of people rarely completely agree on anything so someone must be chosen to decide the answers to important decisions. Because leadership involves choices it brings with it louder criticism, second-guessing, doubts, and even discussions behind your back.

Deciding to lead immediately creates distance between you and the people you seek to lead. Leadership also enables growth, insights, and experiences that those unwilling to lead don't receive. Leadership allows you to see, hear, learn, and feel things you would never encounter if you didn't raise your hand and volunteer yourself as a leader.

Leadership refines individuals. It increases their capacity. It expands their influence and impact. It broadens their legacy. Being a leader is honestly, awesome! There's nothing like making a significant impact on an organization's performance or another person's life.

If you answered Question #1—*Do you want to be a leader?*—with a YES, then you're ready to head to chapter two now.

SOMETIMES THE TIMING ISN'T RIGHT

To those who answered Question #1 with a no, I appreciate your honesty. Perhaps you're overwhelmed with the demands of life right now and taking on additional responsibility isn't something you can muster at this moment in your life. Don't beat yourself up over it. Your moment will come. And when it does I hope you'll return these pages and seize the opportunity to impact others in a broader way.

There is one last group I need to address before we move on to chapter two. Some of you want to lead but feel that someone else is holding you back. You want to contribute more to an organization but when you've applied for a promotion to management you were denied the opportunity or told to go gain more experience and wait your turn.

Listen to me closely. No one can stop you from deciding to lead! Yes, they can block you from the title or position you want in a company but they cannot put you in a box. If they try, consider appropriate ways to contribute more broadly and significantly to the organization. If your well-intentioned and humble efforts are punished then it may be time to consider another place to contribute in a more meaningful way.

Do not allow yourself to become resentful. Do not allow yourself to be stagnant. Bitterness and apathy don't look good on a leader. Use the opportunity to motivate you. Being denied an opportunity to contribute more significantly to an organization can be a gift. It can be the nudge that's needed to knock on another door and discover opportunities to have an impact you currently don't see or aren't considering.

NEXT STEPS

- Answer question #1: Do you want to be a leader?
- Consider the challenges that being a leader will create for you at work, home, and in other areas of your life. Having discussions with family members and friends about the emotional toll a leadership role could have on you is a good idea. Take their insights and thoughts into account as you consider your readiness to lead in a more significant way.
- Start to flex your leadership muscles by volunteering for assignments, offering ideas and solutions, and connecting with as many people as possible. Learn as much as you can about the area you want to lead in. Connect with as many people as possible so you have a broad group to call upon for ideas and feedback as you lead.
- Think about areas you are now demonstrating "maintaining" rather than "leading." Where are you simply maintaining the status quo or managing process or schedules but not truly

leading others? Think about how you could show up differently to demonstrate true leadership.

To read the full book search Amazon.com for Decide to Lead: The Four Questions Anyone Who Wants to Lead Others Must Be Able to Answer

ABOUT THE AUTHORS

RUSS HILL is the host of the Culture Hacks podcast on Apple Podcasts and Spotify. He is one of the authors of *Remoteability: 12 Tactics to Manage the Culture of Your Suddenly Remote Team* and the author of *Decide to Lead: The Four Questions Anyone Who Wants to Lead Others Must Be Able to Answer*. Russ is the father of four children.

JARED JONES is one of the authors of *Remoteability: 12 Tactics to Manage the Culture of Your Suddenly Remote Team* and *Propeller: Accelerating Change by Getting Accountability Right*. Jared is the father of seven kids.

Jared & Russ coach executives at some of the largest companies in the world. They are the co-founders of Lone Rock Consulting.

Interact directly with Russ & Jared at LeadIn30.com or learn more about Lone Rock Consulting at lonerock.io.